A BOY NAMED POOH

A MEMOIR ON HEALING FROM COMPLEX TRAUMA

EVAN HOLT

CONTENTS

Preface v
A Note to the Reader vii
Introduction xi
Section I xiii

1. 'Shakes' 1
2. Early Childhood 5
3. Generational Trauma 11
4. Family Dysfunction 17
5. Fighting My Authoritarian Father 29
6. Failing to Manage my Brother's Dysregulation 35
7. Military Career 41
8. Emotional Intelligence and Hovering a Helicopter 45
9. Inclement Weather and Depression 57
10. Strengthening the Steel 67
11. War and Combat 75
12. Chronic Stress of Combat Operations 81
13. Compounding Unresolved Stresses and Their Effects 89
14. CASEVAC Missions Were the Worst 97
15. Marriage and Blocked Memories 103
16. High-Tempo Overseas Tour 109
17. Twilight Tour 113
18. After Retirement 117

Section II 123
Transformation 125

19. Safety is at the Root of Healing 129
20. Changing My Closed Mind 133
21. Dipping My Toe into Psychedelics 137
22. Expanding my Perspective 143
23. Spiritual Awakening 149
24. Tarot Reading 155
25. Recovered Memories & Internal Family Systems (IFS) Parts Work 161
26. Deeper Dive 171

27. The Power of Journaling 175
28. The Power of the Purge 183
29. My First Ketamine Journey 195
30. Integration 199
Section III 201
'Shakes' Take 203
31. Drug vs Medicine 205
32. The Power of Perspective 211
33. Power of Positive Affirmations 217
34. The 'Inner' Voice 223
35. The Divinity Within and a Higher Power? 229
36. Real Men Don't Cry 233
37. Yoga 239
38. Trauma and Grief 245

Accept Your Fate or Amor Fati 253
Acknowledgments 255

PREFACE

To learn not only who you have become . . . but why, is the greatest gift you can give yourself.

It is empowering . . .

It is freeing . . .

It is calming . . .

And I am Grateful!

It took me fifty years to understand how the abuse and neglect I experienced as a young child instilled patterns and beliefs that negatively affected my whole life . . . until now. Because of this programming, calmness and peace had escaped me my entire life. These beliefs and behaviors, at the time, were successful coping mechanisms that served an initial purpose but, over time, created separation: first from the world and the ones I loved, and eventually from myself. By age fifty, my physical health was suffering, and my mental health was deeply disturbed. I found myself circling the drain. I was desperate to find a way out of the 'Wheel of Pain' that had become my life.

I was blessed to be able to find a way out of my emotional pain without hitting the 'reset button' on life that my parents chose. I was able to find inner peace and love by deeply reflecting on my life through the lens of trauma. During this inner reflective journey to understand how traumatic events had shaped me, I utilized the wisdom of trauma-informed thought leaders (Dr. Gabor Mate, Dr. Bessel van der Kolk, Dr. Richard Schwartz, Dr. Bruce Perry, and others) to deeply examine my life and that of those around me. My ability to understand my emotions and manage them was severely hampered due to not fully processing traumatic events as a child. After college, I joined the Marine Corps, where I served 21 years of active duty as a Cobra attack helicopter pilot, with two combat tours in this role. The high-stress career further contributed to my physical and mental health challenges. After leaving service, my understanding of who I had become was unknown to me due to the dissociative coping mechanism I first utilized as a means of protection against the repeating pattern of generational trauma.

I was blessed to be able to recover and resolve these memories through the proper use of psychedelic medicine under therapeutic conditions. I want to be up front that this memoir is not an argument for psychedelics. It is an argument for healing—and a testimony to the power that psychedelics hold as one path toward healing trauma.

Because I grew up in a very dysfunctional environment, my inward journey to understand who I had become and why was extremely difficult at times. I chose powerful medicines under controlled settings to help me recover lost aspects of myself. Once I broke open my hidden past and the self-defeating behaviors my past had programmed into me, I was able to see the world through a new *perspective*. With my newfound *perspective*, I was able to find and integrate parts of myself I had left behind, thus resolving my actions and behaviors that I did not understand and that no longer served me.

In the end, I found a way to love myself and will be forever grateful for this gift.

With Love,

Evan '*Shakes*' Holt

A NOTE TO THE READER

This educational memoir is based on my personal experiences regarding traumatic events. I wrote this memoir as an exploration of how traumatic events affected me and those around me and as an invitation for you, the reader, to deeply examine your own life experiences. We all have life experiences that program behaviors, beliefs, and coping strategies that make you who you are . . . today. I take you on my journey to reprogram myself to a happier, mentally healthier version. What worked for me may not be right for you; therefore, this memoir is not a prescription but a call to deep, inner reflection. Should you choose any of the tools or methods I selected, I ask that you ensure proper guidance from qualified people and proper safety protocols are in place to ensure success.

Throughout the memoir, I use intentional stylistic choices. I credit much of my transformation journey to the trauma-informed thought leaders' wisdom, which provided me with the foundation for deep self-reflection about how trauma impacted my life.

Dr. Gabor Mate and his book *The Myth of Normal* were instrumental to my journey. I place the word 'normal' in quotation marks as an homage to his teachings. This is deliberate. When I use the term 'normal' in quotations, I am asking you to reflect upon what your 'normal' was growing up, or what you think society's 'normal' is. By examining the differences between all our normals, you will gain a deeper understanding of the human experience, as it has for me. Much of what we think or accept as 'normal' does not universally fit everyone's experiences. By labeling someone's behavior as 'abnormal,' understand whose definition you are using, at what cost, and to whom.

Dr. Richard Schwartz and his Internal Family Systems (IFS) psychotherapeutic model for examining oneself, and his book *No Bad Parts,* were also instrumental in my journey. His model uses the eight C's (*Calmness, Curiosity, Compassion, Confidence, Courage, Clarity, Creativity, and Connectedness*) and five P's (*Presence, Patience, Perspective, Persistence, and Playfulness*) to foster deep inner cognitive reflection and self-examination. This model was extremely important to my self-discovery; therefore, whenever I use any of the C's or P's according to his teachings, I *italicize* them to give him credit.

This memoir weaves between story and insight, memory and meaning. At times, the narrative may feel non-linear. This is not accidental but intentional. Trauma itself is not stored or recalled in a neat timeline; therefore, healing rarely unfolds in straight lines. Some chapters lean into my lived experiences, whereas others are more reflective, offering meaning or additional insight into the effects of those experiences.

Because of this, I separate the memoir into three sections:

Section I: Life History and Background,

Section II: Transformation & Healing Journey, and

Section III: Lessons Learned and Additional Reflections.

If you find yourself drifting, I encourage you to slow down rather than push through. Some of the information presented can be dense or difficult to absorb upon first glance; therefore, it should not be rushed. You may have questions that I answer in later chapters or sections of the book. In some cases, I refer to those chapters in case you want to explore more deeply.

Music was another important aspect of my healing journey, so I sometimes insert lyrics that reflect my feelings at the time. It is my hope that you take the time to listen to some of these songs as a break in the storyline. Music can convey so much more when it comes to emotions or feelings than can be written in text alone.

This memoir was written with honesty from the only perspective I know—my own. I utilize the phrase "*This I Know*" as I reflect on my life's experiences. These are not universal declarations but markers for my personal truths. They may run counter to your truths. I invite you first to listen, then decide for yourself if my truths hold meaning for you . . . or not, as I do not mean to impose my beliefs or truths on you.

What is yours . . . is yours.

What is mine . . . is mine.

As I wind up my *perspective*, I would be remiss if I did not mention that some of the personal experiences of this memoir address difficult material to include: childhood trauma, abuse, addiction, and loss. I have done my best to approach these topics with honesty and *compassion* while trying not to dive so deep that they impart my trauma onto you or sensationalize. Still, I encourage you to take care of yourself as you read. Take breaks when they are needed. Return when you are ready!

Even though this memoir is my very personal look at how traumatic events became trauma for me or those I witnessed. I want you to walk away with a better understanding of not only who *you are*, but also. . .

who you want to become!

In this effort, I ask you to put down your defenses while, at the same time, stepping into your *curiosity*, *compassion*, and *courage*! If you do, your life will become happier, healthier, and kinder. . . as it has for me.

Lastly, know that this memoir was written with love. . . and that, should you choose to walk down this path with me, I would truly be grateful!

This I Know!

INTRODUCTION

We are currently in a worldwide mental health crisis that affects over one billion people. The COVID pandemic exacerbated this crisis through alienation of the people, which has led to a significant increase in anxiety, depression, and loneliness, as well as other mental health conditions. By some statistics, 85% of the global population with mental health challenges do not receive professional care. They go untreated due to the high cost of treatment, local laws and governance, and the complexities that surround their manifestation.

I challenge you to reflect upon your most difficult experiences with *curiosity* and *compassion* so that meaning can be found, as I did. I hope that you will find a *connection* and *clarity* to your own life, which has shaped 'who you or those around you have become.' It is also my hope that you will find comfort in the lessons learned and the methods and tools I utilized, which helped me:

to remember . . .

to understand . . .

to process . . .

and, most importantly, to let go.

I wholeheartedly hope that this book will provide you with deeper insight into your own triggers, traumas, and deep-seated negative feelings so that you might gain the insight and tools to better address them. If you are anything like me, stripping away some of your subconscious or unconscious negative beliefs or behaviors will allow you to become a happier, healthier individual.

If you find yourself or others around you struggling with stress, suffering from anxiety or depression, or more serious mental health dysregulations such as (C)PTSD, then this memoir can help guide you through the challenges and complexities associated with mental health. As I tell my very personal story around trauma and the tools and techniques that I found useful, I weave in many mental health modalities and how they were useful to me so that you can pick and choose the ones that resonate with you. My story, while unique, is universal—therefore applicable to anyone whose life has been touched by a traumatic event or wants to understand trauma to a greater degree.

Recent clinical trials in the U.S. are proving that MDMA and psilocybin, as well as other psychedelic medicines under therapeutic conditions, have the power to reduce or even reverse PTSD symptoms. I used some of these medicines and tools under proper conditions to facilitate my inward journey and discover who I had become. They helped me see myself objectively and become a much happier, healthier person.

By examining your earliest, most painful memories that have shaped who you have become, you, too, can grow and ascend toward your truest and highest Self. *By healing yourself, you are positively improving not only your life but of those you encounter, and thus you are doing your part to heal humanity.*

This I Know!

SECTION I

1

'SHAKES'

All military pilots have a call sign or nickname used over radio traffic; mine was '*Shakes*' because I entered military service with severe hand tremors. Since no medical defect caused my benign tremors, they were not considered disqualifying for my military service. My call sign was a running joke within my squadrons. My fellow pilots would joke that the only reason I was any good at flying the helicopter (AH-1W) and at delivering weapons was because both the aircraft and I shook at the same rate (amplitude) but in an opposite pattern (out of phase), so our shaking would cancel each other out. We would joke that if I ever crashed my helicopter, it would probably be because our shaking got synchronized (in phase), which would cause my shaking to make the aircraft fall apart.

Yes, my tremors were that bad. I would give briefings to new people, and they would see me shaking like a leaf, but because my call sign was '*Shakes*,' everyone gave me a pass. My shaking was so intense that it masked how often I was especially nervous when briefing flights. This worked to my benefit. For every negative, there is a positive.

I have experienced this shaking for as long as I can remember: It is all I have ever known.

I thought my shaking was due to a genetic trait I inherited from my father. He also shook, but to a much lesser degree than I do. It wasn't until I was fifty-four years old that I realized my shaking was not due to a genetically inherited trait but due to generational trauma.

People who knew of my military service and saw my shaking assumed it was due to PTSD from my military experiences. I told them I did not have PTSD, and I would explain that I have had these tremors since I was a small child. They had nothing to do with PTSD . . . or so I thought.

Before I begin telling the story of my childhood, I want to make clear that I am not a victim. I do not hold any hate, resentment, or ill will toward the man who abused me at a very young age. That man was my father. In fact, if I could give him and his wounded parts a giant hug, I would do so lovingly and with the utmost *compassion*. He, like every person on this planet, *only knew what he knew when he knew it.* I would love to share my love with him, but that is not possible. Unfortunately, he took his own life in August 2002 when I was a Captain in the Marine Corps. He took his life just under a year after my mom died of liver failure due to her alcoholism. Both killed themselves, but from opposite ends of the suicide spectrum. One through her inability to end the long-established pattern of 'checking out' from her emotions through the consumption of alcohol. One deliberately because the actions of his life became overwhelming when he began to examine them. *Both through their inability to control their pain*

I also want to convey that I am one of the most blessed individuals to walk this planet. I have been fortunate to travel extensively. I have been to six continents and approximately forty countries, and have been able to share and engage in conversation with people from totally different cultures, religions, and ideas; all of which have opened my mind and provided me with a very broad *perspective* on the human experience. I have seen some of the best of humanity; I have also seen some of the worst. *Everything in my life has brought me to where I am now.*

I feel blessed to have had such difficult and disturbing experiences, which provided me with my teachings and unique perspective, which prepared me and made me uniquely qualified to write about trauma in broad terms. *These difficult experiences made me better, stronger, and more understanding of how traumatic events can shape one's life. They also came at a cost . . . due to my own shortcomings. I held on to the anger, pain, sorrow, and negative thoughts and emotions associated with some of these experiences . . . much of which I even hid from myself.*

This I Know!

2

EARLY CHILDHOOD

Traumatic events happen to everyone . . . eventually. Trauma is what happens in the body. Trauma is distress without resolution, which causes emotional dysregulation and imprints on the body. This is how my unresolved trauma affected me for 50 years.

I was born on October 28th, 1969, with underdeveloped lungs and severe asthma. Studies regarding mothers under chronic stress during pregnancy show that this stress can be passed to the child in vitro and can manifest as asthma as part of the emerging understanding of epigenetics. I now know that my father hit my mother when he was drunk, and when she was pregnant with me. In addition, my mother smoked cigarettes while pregnant. So, one or the other, or the combination of both, caused my severe asthma.

Growing up, both my parents smoked about a pack of cigarettes a day, and they did most of it in our home or car, which, unfortunately, would trigger severe asthma attacks in me. As an infant and small child, there were many times that my parents rushed me to the hospital emergency room, because I would get a severe asthma attack. My breathing would get so shallow and constricted that they thought I might die. I would have a deeply croupy, shallow wheeze. On a few occasions, I would be kept in the hospital for a few days to a week at a time, where the crib I was placed in had an oxygen tent surrounding it and me. The doctors put me in an elevated oxygen environment to keep my oxygen saturation level high enough and long enough to recover.

One of the unfortunate side effects of severe asthma in preschoolers is extended bed wetting. Unfortunately, this was not known to my parents, so when it came time for me to stop wetting my diaper, I wasn't progressing as my older siblings had, nor according to the 'normal' schedule. Because I was not progressing properly, my father decided he was going to spank the bed wetting out of me. Unfortunately, my father's definition of a spanking was with his belt, and he did it with anger and rage all too often. He felt I was just a lazy child who didn't care enough to wake up, get out of bed, and use the toilet.

He quickly got frustrated that the spankings were not working, so the belt whippings became harder, and the words associated with The Belt got harsher. My dad's belt was a thick strap of leather with two continuous rows of holes running the entire length. So, wherever The Belt struck, it left a distinctive pattern of small red circles or blood blisters, serving as a warning to the other siblings. Because physical and verbal punishment were the only tools in my father's parenting toolbox, the beltings continued to the point where I was being woken up out of a deep sleep to him screaming at me for wetting the sheets.

On October 28th, 2023, and for my fifty-fourth birthday, I decided that I did not want to celebrate or be with others, but do a cognitive deep dive utilizing psychedelic medicine, specifically psilocybin and MDMA. The reason I did not want to celebrate or be with others was that by this point in my life, I was mostly closed off to the world. In fact, I was closed off so much so that my wife and I had separated a few years earlier due to my anger and emotional unavailability. I was angry at a lot of things, including her excessive alcohol consumption and how she seemed to be following in my mother's footsteps. I was powerless to convince her to stop, and I felt like a failure because of it. I was mostly "*closed off*" to the world, including my family, and, if I am being completely truthful, I was shutting down to myself as well, and this was an attempt to understand how I got 'here.'

During this birthday '*inner work*,' and as I took the psychedelic medicine. I said aloud my intention: *Why did I have a visceral fear and hatred for my father by the time I entered kindergarten?"* I knew I had a significant fear of him by the time I entered school, but I didn't remember or know why, because I had blocked out much of my youth. So, I put extreme safety measures in place, such as locking my keys in a safe and placing notes on the exterior doors to ensure I would not leave my house or the four corners of my property. After I felt comfortable in creating an environment I knew I could feel safe in, I utilized psilocybin and MDMA to facilitate this journey inward. At the time, these drugs were, and still are, illegal in the United States. However, this medicine unblocked my early childhood memories and gave them back to me with such clarity that I could see the visuals . . . I could feel the pain . . . and I could sense the rush of panic that the three-year-old version of myself felt as if they were happening in the present.

Yes, they were that powerful and clear!

The first memory that flooded back into my consciousness was me, a three-year-old, being awoken by my father, who stood over me.

As I open my eyes and am awoken from a dead sleep. I see my father standing over me. He pulls my top sheet and bedspread off me. *RAGE* is quickly boiling up in his face as the vein in his forehead begins to swell and pulse. He screams at me while grabbing me by my left wrist. He flings my three-year-old self out of bed and harshly against the cabinets that lined the wall beside my bed. My back hits one of the vertical handles that sat atop each cabinet door. As I am recalling this memory, I feel the actual pain of the handle poking me in my upper left shoulder as if it is happening in the present. My three-year-old self tumbles and then looks up at him from the ground. Immediately, I can feel that version of me is in a state of panic as I see my father standing over me, pointing at the wet sheets and screaming at me.

He was screaming things like *"You lazy fucking child, what the fuck is wrong with you?"* and other hurtful and hateful words. As he was screaming at me, he removed his belt and then proceeded to repeatedly strike me with The Belt. I try to squirm to avoid it, but, in all honesty, it only makes it worse. He yells at me to stop moving as he whips me with

RAGE! By the end, I looked like I had severe chickenpox on my legs, arms, and face, due to the holes in the belt leaving round, red circles wherever they landed. I was crying and saying, *"No, Daddy, please. . . No . . . I don't know why I wet the bed; I will be better."*

WOW!

I have never had such a vivid memory in all my life as the one that was given back to me after I asked myself this important question. I, NOW, fully understood why I feared my father so deeply and so early in my life and how hurtful and hateful he had been to me. To get this memory back, as you can imagine, was quite startling, and it took me several weeks to fully understand and process it. I discuss in detail in Section II.

I locked away this event, and many others like it, hidden inside of me for fifty years. My inability to recall these events, along with the associated coping mechanisms, such as disassociation and hypervigilance, allowed me to endure the ensuing and future repetitive events to a much greater degree. This is my understanding of how PTSD manifested in me.

Recent psychological studies have shown a link between emotional stress and bed wetting in early youth and pre-adolescent children. So, my father's actions actually made the problem worse, not better. As we used to joke in the Marine Corps, the beatings shall continue until morale improves. The difference was that, in the Marine Corps, this was a joke to provide *perspective*. As in—it could actually be worse. But in the case of my three-year-old self, this trauma became my 'on and off' daily reality for years.

Thus, my trauma, or what is generally accepted as Complex PTSD, began around the age of three, and prevented me from remembering the story of much of my childhood until I unlocked these memories at the end of 2023, utilizing psychedelic medicine for therapeutic purposes. I locked away this memory, and many more like it, until I was fifty-four years old.

Some of my coping mechanisms served me well, like hyper-vigilance. These beatings made me pay attention to everything around me, which set me up for success later in life. Other coping mechanisms, like disassociation, closed me off emotionally, which imprinted a sense of aloneness in the world and filled my head with an internal dialogue of self-beratement for every mistake I made.

Once I unlocked these memories and provided my much younger self the love and compassion he desperately needed five decades prior, I was able to free myself from my own verbal self-abuse. *Once free from this internal abuse, it allowed me to love myself and—by extension—to be able to start to show and share my love with others.*

This I Know!

3

GENERATIONAL TRAUMA

Generational trauma is the harmful effects of historical mistreatment or abuse. The symptoms of these traumas are passed down from generation to generation. Much of who we become stems from early childhood and how unresolved Big 'T' or little 't' traumas are passed on from generation to generation.

What we do not resolve, we repeat.

To understand how my father, who was such an intelligent and successful businessman, could behave the way he did, one must understand his childhood and the traumatic events that shaped his life and behavior. My father was significantly abused and neglected as a small child himself. He grew up very poor, and both of his parents were severe alcoholics. I do not know much about my dad's mom because she died of alcoholism and cancer when I was very young. I remember my grandfather to some degree. He was a tough man, distrustful of the government, and a heavy drinker. I know that my grandfather tried to kill my dad not once . . . but twice. Both times, my grandfather was in an alcoholic rage. The first time was before I was born, and my dad forgave his father. He excused his father's behavior as a 'one-off' blacked-out rage event. The second time was during a family visit to my grandfather's house. I honestly do not remember much from the incident other than my grandfather took out a gun and threatened my father with it. They exchanged harsh words, and we left in a hurry. As we left Mosby, Missouri, and drove home to Lawrence, Kansas, my father became overwhelmed with rage. He became madder and madder the more he drove. In other words, he locked in and embodied this pain!

That was the last time I saw my grandfather. We never went to visit again, and we didn't even go to his funeral. In fact, any time my grandfather's name was mentioned, my dad would get triggered and scream at us to never mention his name again because he was *"DEAD TO (HIM)."*

My dad's parents abused and neglected him enough at a young age that his grandmother ended up taking him from his parents and raising him herself by the time he was seven or eight. Unfortunately, a lot of the developmental emotional regulatory damage had already been done.

The first five years of a child's development are extremely formative for the child's emotional baseline, which extends into adulthood. Dr. Bruce Perry's book titled *The Boy Who Was Raised as a Dog* does an excellent job explaining how early neglect and trauma can manifest in different behavior depending upon the timing and age. This early extreme neglect and abuse set the conditions for my father's emotional dysregulation for the rest of his life.

During my early adult life, my mom, siblings, and I used to joke that our dad was an 'emotional infant'. What I now know is that my father was emotionally stunted as an infant or somewhere very early in his childhood, and *he never properly processed his trauma.* He, like many people of his generation, locked his trauma deep inside his subconscious and never sought or believed in mental health therapy. In other words, he had PTSD from a very early age, and he unwittingly passed it on to me because *'When we don't resolve— We repeat their patterns.'*

My father's unresolved trauma and subsequent emotional dysregulation drove him to behave the way he did. His father's hurtful and hateful words became his words, which then became my words . . . to myself.

If you recognize aspects of your upbringing or the upbringing of loved ones that have similar generational trauma markers, I challenge you to treat yourself or your loved ones with *compassion* and love. "*Only through love can past traumas and triggers be released.*"

Shame, beratement, and anger only serve to lock these behaviors in. Understand that these behaviors come from a wounded part of yourself or your loved one that has yet to receive resolution. In many instances, you or your loved one may not even recognize or understand where these behaviors originate. I know I didn't!

If it is a loved one, you cannot fix them; only they can fix themselves. If it is yourself, you must go back to that earlier version of yourself and go into yourself, to get through the original distress without resolution. *You must address this earlier part of yourself with love and compassion to resolve what disturbs you to begin with.*

This is why MDMA, aka the love drug, is so effective against trauma resolution. By finding a way to love or fully accept everything that has happened—to you or by you—only then can you remove the emotional distress they imprinted in you. *Once you have fully resolved the experience, you eliminate the behaviors that caused you to be emotionally activated or 'triggered' to begin with.*

This dysregulation can manifest as anxiety, escapism (flight), anger or rage (fight), shame, and guilt, among others. Do not blame others for your shortcomings; instead, look within to address the unresolved parts of your past. Once you have resolved your own challenges, you might find the compassion for those who created them, and perhaps only then can you help them find resolution.

If you, the reader, grew up in a much less chaotic environment, this does not mean that you do not have small yet significant events (small 't' traumas) from your childhood that have instilled self-limiting or self-defeating behaviors. Our brains are constantly developing all the way through young adulthood and age twenty-five and beyond, so *the earlier in life you have a potentially traumatic event, and where you are in life, and the brain's development are critical to how well one can understand . . . thus process.*

Becoming aware of and understanding these aspects of your early life will give you great insight into how the world has shaped you into who you are. We all have childhood or early adult experiences that have imprinted on our subconscious, making us who we are. If you find yourself having an emotional response to a seemingly mundane interaction or experience, that is exactly what I am referring to. This is called an autonomic nervous system activation and is part of your emotional default mode network.

In my journey to understand my behaviors, I learned that these emotional reactions are automatic and uncontrollable without resetting the underlying distress that triggers their subconscious activation. Some of these triggers or disturbances in our subconscious occur due to adult traumatic experiences. These are much easier to identify. You might find yourself surprised, as I was, that much of who you have become results from your early childhood.

This is because, as a small child (0-5), the prefrontal cortex, which is responsible for higher-level thinking, reasoning, and emotional regulation, is only a framework, with little capacity to analyze its environment. How can it? A small child doesn't have enough life experience to determine whether what is being shown to them is just or good. This part of the brain has not yet developed, and what little is formed gets turned off during times of extreme stress as part of the sympathetic fight-or-flight response.

Depending on the timing of the traumatic event, different emotional dysregulations can be imprinted or avoided. What may not be traumatic for a fully mature adult may be extremely traumatic for a young child. Dr. Bruce Perry's book *"The Boy Who Was Raised as a Dog"* does an excellent job of detailing how trauma can affect the young mind, and I highly recommend it if any of this information resonates with you.

So, as small children, most of what we perceive is taken at 'face value' with no real analysis of what happened or why. To a large degree, we just record and accept what we are being shown. If you are told you are bad or stupid, or smart or good, these self-identities get ingrained into your subconscious. So, depending on what you are shown during this early portion of programming, your life will manifest as different ideas, beliefs, or behaviors.

I challenge you to examine your early life. What are your beliefs about yourself? Where did they come from? What do you think your parents thought about themselves, and which of those traits were programmed into you, yet don't truly represent who you are as a person?

I challenge you to make the conscious effort to examine whether generational small 't' traumas are creating limiting self-beliefs or activating certain negative emotions, thereby limiting your happiness or mental health.

I challenge you to examine the chart below, which compares divine vs wounded traits, and ask yourself which traits resonate with your own actions or those of the people you interact with.

Divine	**Wounded**
Receptive	Closed off
Encouraging	Aggressive
Trusts Self	Poor Boundaries
Grounded	Insecure
Nurturing	Manipulative
Clear Communication	Defensive
Empowered	Victimized

Use this chart, or search the internet for Divine/Wounded—Masculine/Feminine to examine and determine how you or others reacted or responded in a particular situation. If your actions align with the wounded side, this indicates there is a wounded part of you that needs addressing . . . thus, resolve.

Find a way into these early and deep-seated memories, feelings, or triggers. Find a way to understand—to accept, and to resolve within yourself. This 'inner work' can be extremely tough and can be very painful, as it was for me, but it is the only way I have found to fully break the cycle of generational or early trauma. *You must go in and go through . . . in order to get out.*

Do not blame. Do not judge. Do not berate yourself or others. These actions only perpetuate the hurt. It is the hurt, the hate, and the resentment that need to be resolved within ourselves. This hurt and hate can be directed at someone else or inward, as it was for me. Both of these beliefs hold you back, preventing your progress toward a happier, healthier version of yourself.

This I Know!

4

FAMILY DYSFUNCTION

The definition of a dysfunctional family is any family with more than one person. We are all imperfect human beings; therefore, imperfect actions and reactions happen every day, with misunderstandings at every turn. Understanding and accepting the imperfections in all of us helps facilitate our resolution of emotional distress within ourselves and others, paving the way toward healing.

My father believed that the reason his parents fought and drank so much was due to being poor. So, he worked really, really hard to make sure his family wasn't poor. He was very successful at climbing the economic ladder, but, unfortunately, he failed to address much, if any, of his trauma or childhood distress.

Late in his life, my dad confessed to my older sister that he remembers crying in his crib due to soiling his diapers, and his parents wouldn't check on him for hours. He believed his parents never loved him. This left tremendous emotional scars on his own sense of self-worth, and I believe that he never loved himself, either. He never properly processed his early childhood trauma, so all too often, he would easily get triggered and would fly into a fit of anger and rage.

My dad's unconscious emotional dysregulation would get triggered and cause him to fly into a rage on what seemed to be a daily basis. It wasn't daily, but was often enough that my family would 'walk on eggshells' around him so that we wouldn't do anything to activate his emotional dysregulation and get punished by his rage. When he was triggered, it didn't matter who he was mad at; anyone in his path would feel his RAGE. My family even had a nickname for his dysregulated behavior. We called it the '*Wrath of Ron.*' Unfortunately, my father's unresolved childhood trauma created a very stressful family dynamic. We all were afraid of him, my mom included.

When my dad would drink, he would get very abusive . . . just like his father would. In fact, it got so bad that we were removed from the home by extended family shortly after I started school. To save the marriage, my father stopped drinking and consequently stopped hitting my mother, but because it was considered discipline, he continued to hit his children. For the rest of his life, he 'white knuckled' his pain.

My mother did her best to protect us from his wrath, but she was too small to confront him directly. Instead, she threaded our trauma and pain into her heart. Since mental health therapy was considered unacceptable, my mother tried to drown her feelings and emotions with alcohol, to hide them away, even from herself. She drank herself to liver failure, knowing for years that this was to be her death should she continue. She died two weeks after September 11, 2001, at the age of sixty-one.

I am grateful for the love my mother showed me, as it was her love that allowed me to distance myself somewhat from my internal verbal abuse and to project love outwardly, even though I struggled with love internally. I knew she loved me even though I never felt loved by my father; one is much better than none, as was the case for my father.

For me, the frequent hard beatings with The Belt clearly sent the message that wetting the bed was not acceptable. Since I did not know where my bed wetting manifested from, I had to deploy tactics to try to reduce these harsh reminders of my inadequacies. I did not want to be a lazy child. I did not want to be screamed and whipped with a belt for being bad, so I became *hyper-focused* and *hyper-vigilant* of my actions and the actions of those around me.

My mistakes hurt, so I paid closer attention to the details of everything around me. Over the next couple of years, I learned to avoid drinking any fluids late in the day; I focused on staying up as late as I could, then going to the bathroom at the last second before falling asleep. Unfortunately, on some occasions, I fell asleep before using the bathroom, so another whipping would commence.

My hyper-vigilance turned my 'beltings' into a game. What did I do wrong this time? I drank too late . . . Ok, noted. One point for my father. On days when I didn't wet the bed, one point for me. I employed many strategies, from sleeping on towels or several layers of dirty clothes to absorb my mistakes. I would even keep a quick change of pajamas in the cabinets right next to the bed, so I could change into them before my father came in to check on me. This strategy worked well . . . until it didn't. He noticed I was wearing different pajamas, and rage overtook him. He dished out an extra poignant dose of discipline to ensure I got the message.

The next strategy I tried was to sleep naked in a sleeping bag and in my closet. I had my clean pajamas next to me, and I would put them on in the morning and climb into my bed. This new strategy worked well . . . until it didn't. He found me still naked and asleep in my sleeping bag. He yanked me from my sleeping bag and gave me an impassioned and hard punishment across most of my naked body, which left blood blisters wherever they landed. In this moment, I quickly learned how much my thin pajamas had protected me so many times before. It was so bad that my mom couldn't send me to school for a few days because she "couldn't send me to school looking like that."

I even slept on a piece of linoleum that I saved from one of my dad's construction projects until my father found me before I woke up. Once again, he proceeded to whip me with rage because I was trying to *"CHEAT!"* In my mind, I wasn't trying to cheat but survive . . . what did my four- or five-year-old brain know?

About the same time, I became enthralled with the book *Winnie the Pooh*. In fact, when people would say my name, I would respond with, "Me no Evan, me Pooh."

I became Pooh for the next several years to mentally separate myself from the bad child that Evan was. In other words, I disassociated from myself.

The book is about a bear of little brains who struggles to understand what is going on around him. Looking back, *Winnie the Pooh* allowed me to disassociate from the world around me because I was not wise enough to understand why things were unfolding the way they were. I was powerless to fully affect their outcome; therefore, this book allowed me to trust and believe in myself while, at the same time, disassociate from the abuse. My love for this book and my subsequent character disassociation gave me the courage to play the game with my father, thus creating distance between myself and my internal critical *'Voice of Deratement'* for being a half-wit bear.

Later, as an adult, this 'Voice of Beratement' was just a moment away, residing in my subconscious. Anytime I made a mistake, my internal critical voice popped into my consciousness, harshly pointing out the *'MISTAKE'* and berating me for it. I would internally scream at myself for being lazy or not paying attention to something. While it created my drive and success, it was exhausting and abusive!!

It appeared that my older brother had a similar 'Voice of Beratement' that he grew up with, only my brother seemed to fully believe all the harsh words as if these words were his own and who he was. For some reason, I understood that these words were not my highest or truest 'Self,' so this voice of beratement didn't fully overtake me. This is the point at which my brother and I diverged in our responses to this 'shared reality' and in the subsequent behaviors that followed. He did not get the gift of emotional disassociation as I had. My brother sternly internalized his hatred and shame for himself, just like my father had, and as he imprinted on us. I was blessed to be the one to 'somewhat avoid' or distance myself from this pitfall.

I will be forever grateful for this blessing.

Over time, the beltings got easier because I learned not to squirm and just take them. By learning not to squirm or fight back, I avoided further damage to sensitive areas like the backs of my hands and my face. I was powerless to stop them, so I hardened my mental attitude toward them. As a young child, when I would witness my older siblings getting The Belt, I would cry and tremble for them. My dad would yell, "Why are you crying?" or "I'll give you something to really cry about!"

These hateful words were probably his father's hateful words to him as a small child as well. So, at a very young age, I started to learn to repress my emotions and to control my crying response. I quickly found out that not crying was the wrong answer, so I learned to hold my cry until the right time. I found that if I started to cry after a few strikes, it had the greatest effect under 'normal' circumstances.

The more my father was triggered, and the more he was in the state of RAGE, the longer I had to wait to cry. If I cried too early when he was still rageful, it fueled his rage! If I waited too long to cry, he would notice I wasn't crying . . . he would hit me harder. It was the game I had to play with my father for years to lessen the punishment. This set me down a path for most of my life, where I believed emotions were dangerous and that I should do everything in my power to control them.

So, what did I do with those tears?

I did what my mother had done and effectively taught me. I stuffed my tears and repressed the associated emotions down in my subconscious out of the way, so they didn't interfere with my conscious mind . . . or so I thought.

In fact, as an adult, I only cried a couple of times and always alone. This was one of the worst coping mechanisms I employed that negatively affected my life . . . up until recently. I discuss in detail later.

Additionally, as a very young child, I would start to tremble whenever I witnessed my older siblings getting The Belt. When it was my older siblings' turn, I would shake with fear at what I was witnessing, and my father would turn to me and say, "Do you want The Belt?" or "What's your problem?"

I quickly learned that I needed to mask my fear, so I stuffed my emotions even deeper and forced myself not to shake. I turned off my shaking response due to fear, only, instead of shaking when I was scared, I started shaking all the time, and 'Shakes' was born. My constant shaking masked my fear of my father just like it masked my nervousness early in my Marine Corps career. As I mentioned earlier, for every negative there is a positive.

So up until around the age of 9 or 10, I would receive repeated spankings with The Belt from my dysregulated father. My mother would help me hide the bed wetting for certain periods, which would allow my dad's hyper-vigilance to stand down and to focus elsewhere until something happened and he was once again hyper-focused on teaching me how inadequate I was. My mom did the best she could. Unfortunately, she was 4'11" and around 100 pounds, and my dad was about 6 feet and 200 pounds, so she was powerless to confront him directly, and when she did, he would turn on her as well.

My brother is 2.5 years older than I am. He was an emotionally sensitive child, which is why he was affected by the chronic stress of home life to a greater extent than I was. In fact, years later, my older sister told me that he always started to cry 'on the backswing.' In my opinion, his emotional sensitivity led to his struggles with learning . . . and in life. He struggled with learning because of his young age (one of the youngest in his grade) when entering school, and the chronic stress of a very dysfunctional home caused by an abusive father.

He entered kindergarten about the same time I was supposed to stop wetting the bed. We shared a bedroom so he would see me routinely get spanked with anger or rage on many mornings before he would go to school. On occasion, my father's violence would spill over to him. As I look back on his life through the lens of trauma, I think this significantly contributed to his inability to learn. How could he go to school and learn when he had witnessed or been part of a traumatic event that morning? He was helpless to help me and paralyzed by fear of my father's rage turning on him.

My brother struggled to learn in school and was especially bad at math. He was having difficulty learning his multiplication tables in the 2nd

grade. My dad would quiz him with flashcards, and I would sit near them and pay attention. I paid attention because I did not want to go through the emotional pain my brother was experiencing at the time. Many times, my brother would get yelled at for not answering the question correctly, and my dad would say, "What are you, stupid?"

I knew my brother wasn't stupid . . . he was scared! Unfortunately, my brother didn't understand this! At this young and impressionable age, those words ingrained a negative sense of self-worth into my brother, which I am not sure he has resolved to this day.

He would freeze up and couldn't give my dad an answer, afraid of getting it wrong. Since I had been hyper-vigilant the last year or so and I had turned down my emotional stress response, I was able to learn the multiplication tables as well, if not better than my brother had. I was able to learn them because I was not under the duress of the 'hot seat.'

In fact, I knew my multiplication tables by the time I entered kindergarten. On occasion, I would give the right answer when I could see my older brother freeze. This, unfortunately, only served to reinforce my brother's sense of being mentally deficient. So, my brother began to take his frustrations out on me. For most of my childhood, my brother lied to me, stole from me, and of course . . . beat me up. I not only had to guard myself from my father but also from my older brother. As you can imagine, this guarded behavior separated me from having meaningful relationships with others growing up. If you can't trust your own family, who can you trust?

When I was in the fifth grade, and during one of my dad's fits of rage, I stepped between my father and my older brother during one of their arguments. I don't remember what the argument was about, probably grades or something my brother did not do well. I remember my dad yelling at my brother and berating him verbally. My brother popped back with a snide comment, which sent my dad into a POWERFUL RAGE. Immediately, my dad takes off to catch my brother and beat him, but my brother slips by. I was afraid that my dad was going to kill my brother because he was triggered to a level well beyond the 'normal'. I slowed my dad down by stepping in front of him, and without a thought or care, he struck me in the face with his fist.

CRACK! He broke my nose.

It was worth it. My brother escaped to the outside, and he stayed away for several hours until he knew it was safe to come home. My mom never took me to the hospital, and I never received medical care because she was afraid of what would happen to the family if the outside world knew.

My mom, like many people, crafted a very polished façade of perfectness. She made sure we all had the right hair, the right clothes, and the right social behaviors so that the world would see our family through a completely different *perspective.* Outside looking in, we looked better than most. Inside looking out was fraught with chaos and pain at every turn.

I started to hit puberty shortly after getting my nose broken. Recent psychology studies have found that violence and trauma in childhood accelerate puberty and brain development in boys. What I know is that I was the first boy in my class to hit puberty, and my ability to understand complex ideas for my age was keen due to this biological aging mechanism.

This early development set me up for success against my peers in sports and academics in junior high and high school, so I am grateful for this blessing. This is an example of Stoicism's principle of *Fate as a Teacher.* Instead of seeing life's challenges as merely negative, Stoics view them as opportunities for growth and wisdom. Adversity shapes character. In embracing fate, you are also embracing the process of becoming wiser, more resilient, and more virtuous, thereby freeing you from suffering.

As I was starting to age out of my bed wetting, my older sister was entering high school. She didn't have much guidance on how to deal with the chronic stress at home, so she chose the outlet that most kids fall into—drinking alcohol and smoking marijuana. My father was also an authoritarian type of father, so promiscuity was also a factor. She used alcohol and marijuana to numb the stress of home life and looked to boys to get the love she never received from our father.

It wasn't that he didn't love us. He did the best he could. He couldn't show us love because he couldn't love himself—but we couldn't understand this, not as children. Even now, even as I try to understand and untangle my father's psychology, I struggle to fully comprehend the pain he must have felt.

Fast forward a few years, and my brother was now in high school. By this time, his struggles in school were significant, and he was introduced to cocaine. Because we grew up in a highly stressful environment where he was scared most every day that my father was around, I believe he had suppressed dopamine levels.

As recent clinical studies have shown, children who grow up in a chronically stressful environment tend to have suppressed dopamine levels. The body regulates this neurotransmitter to a lower 'at stasis' level because it can't remain elevated or 'on alert' all the time. Those with suppressed dopamine levels are much more susceptible to addiction to drugs such as cocaine and methamphetamines. A great book that addresses this phenomenon is *Dopamine Nation* by Dr. Anna Lemke.

What I do know is that cocaine quickly became my brother's drug of choice.

In the late spring of my eighth-grade year, I was finishing a very successful year in school. Since I had developed earlier than my peers, I was especially strong and athletic; I played four sports and was a starting player in each. By this point, my brother had moved to the basement, and I was still in our once-shared bedroom on the second floor.

TRIGGER WARNING: Animal death

One evening, I am in my bedroom, and I hear a loud '*BANG*.' I go out of my bedroom and walk down to the landing between the basement and second floor of our split-level home to see where the sound came from. I see my beloved dog come running, whining and whimpering as he runs up the stairs toward me. I am confused as to why he is whimpering. I am literally trying to figure out what is happening, as much as my dog is trying to figure out what just happened to him. I sit down, and he comes up to me. I start to pet him and notice he is wet, then I notice he is wet with blood, and he quickly bled out.

My dog died that night because my brother was playing with a gun while high on cocaine. Luckily, my father was out of town on a business trip; otherwise, I am not sure my brother would still be alive. Our dog was about the only thing my dad could show unconditional love to. He was beloved by all of us as he was our entire family's emotional support animal. We all feared our father, my mom included, and what his emotional response would be, should he learn the truth. So, we all concocted and colluded on the story that our dog got hit by a car. We buried him in the backyard before my father returned from his trip to hide the evidence.

Afterwards, the carpet at the top of the landing was permanently stained with blood, and no matter what we did, we could not remove the stain. My dad was extremely frugal, so he decided to cut out the blood-stained area of the carpet. He replaced it with a diamond-shaped patch of linoleum, about two feet on each side.

So, for the next 7 years, every time I walked up and down those stairs, that linoleum diamond reminded me of the tragic event that took place and what it felt like to witness my dog's death. These daily reminders served to reinforce the pain, sorrow, and anger I felt at the time of his death while ingraining the belief that drugs were bad and I should do everything in my power to avoid them. Unfortunately, my brain wasn't developed enough, nor did I have the coping skills to address and resolve these mental disturbances. Instead, I shoved the feelings of anger and sadness down and out of my consciousness. They sat repressed and unresolved in my subconscious for 40 years.

This event, as you can imagine, weighed heavily on my brother. It was obvious that he berated himself, felt extreme shame for what he did, and carried that shame into his adult life, manifesting as many self-defeating behaviors. Looking back, this is where his emotional dysregulation really worsened, and his bipolar-like behavior started to fully exhibit itself.

Later in life, during one of the times I went to visit my brother at an alcohol and drug treatment center, he confessed how he felt so much anger and shame for himself that he couldn't look himself in the mirror. He stated that at the time, it had been years since he had been able to look at himself in a mirror without guilt, shame, or disgust overtaking him.

Knowing what I know now, I wish I were better equipped to help release him from this mental prison. Unfortunately, at the time, I was stuck in my own prison because I, too, had not begun to process many of our shared life events.

While I was able to recall this story and even joke about how screwed up the event was, I failed to fully process this traumatic event. My mother, my siblings, and I were so worried about how my dad would react that none of us fully or properly mourned our dog's death.

In June 2023—forty years later—I finally resolved this disturbance in my state of consciousness by utilizing psychedelic medicine (psilocybin and MDMA) under therapeutic protocols. Under their effects, I finally allowed myself the softness to cry and fully mourn his loss. *With those tears, I was able to let go of much of the pain and sorrow that sat repressed and unprocessed in my subconscious.*

This I Know!

5

FIGHTING MY AUTHORITARIAN FATHER

An authoritarian father is a parent who uses strict rules, high expectations, and punishment to control their child's behavior. Authoritarian fathers may be described as dictatorial and overbearing.

By the time I was in ninth grade, I had been introduced to alcohol and drugs. I knew that if I did partake, my father would get triggered and severely punish me as he did to my older siblings when they were caught. There was a part of me that deeply needed the pain relief they provide. There was another part of me that was keenly aware that I risked unwanted behavior, such as accidentally killing my dog, if I delved too deeply into them. There could be significant and painful repercussions from engaging in them that I did not want.

So, I did what my mother's dad had taught me from a young age. As a young child, I learned two things from him. My mom would get mad at him each time he said these things to me, so I knew they must be important to remember.

The first: "Take her easy . . . and if she's easy . . . take her twice!"

I now understand why my mother felt this might be inappropriate for a young child to hear.

The second: "Be good. If you can't be good, then be good at it."

Be good or be good at it? As a small child who wet the bed for reasons I didn't understand and couldn't seem to control, and who couldn't seem to be good, I figured I was going to have to be *'Good at it.'*

There was a part of me that genuinely and desperately needed the stress relief that drugs and alcohol provide. If I were to utilize this coping mechanism, I knew I had to be 'good at it.' This meant that if I were to partake in drinking and smoking marijuana, I had to do it sparingly and with control. So, I did a little drinking and smoking marijuana in junior high and high school to cope with the extreme stress of home life. In junior high, I drank and smoked with another kid who hit puberty early and was from a very dysfunctional family as well.

Because I couldn't drink alcohol or smoke marijuana very often, this forced me to sit alone in my bedroom and reflect on my thoughts and emotions. Turned out this was a blessing for me as it kept me from 'checking out' through these means. Unfortunately, my friend depended more and more on the coping mechanism of 'checking out' through alcohol and marijuana, and we drifted apart as soon as we hit high school. This self-reflection 'inner work' helped me become cognitively aware at a young age, and I processed much of what I could remember and understand with my still-developing adolescent brain. As a teen who was distrustful of the world, I spent many days alone. This time alone allowed me to reflect inwardly; thus, it steered me away from the drug and alcohol trapping that many disturbed youths fall into: I am grateful for its blessing.

While sitting in my room as a teenager, I often struggled with questions about my father. How does such an intelligent man behave in such a violent and destructive way . . . and to his family, whom he is supposed to love? I sat in my bedroom, alone, for many hours of many days, wrestling with questions like this. In other words, I hid in my bedroom away from my father and brother, and, by extension, I hid from the world because I didn't understand it and felt as though I didn't 'fit in' or belong. I felt alone and different from those around me. It was very difficult for my not fully developed adolescent brain to understand my father's and now my brother's erratic behaviors.

I didn't fully realize how much emotional pain I held onto until September of 2025 and two years into my healing journey, when I was in a therapy session, and the therapist had me revisit my time alone in my bedroom as a teen. A flood of emotions, like loneliness, emptiness, and unworthiness, came flooding back with such force that it became emotionally overwhelming. Even more than revisiting much of my physical abuse had been. In this moment, I realized I had been so focused on the physical abuse that I failed to see the emotional neglect I endured as a small child and its impact on me. While I was able to discuss my physical abuse and trauma without emotional activation easily, I had not yet begun unpacking or addressing the emotional neglect I felt when I was alone and hid in my bedroom forty-plus years ago. We all have blind spots that may require personal or professional help to see ourselves objectively. This is why I am a huge advocate of mental health therapists, wholeness retreats, and the divine work they do.

When I entered high school, I began to pull away from the few friends I had and invested my time in gymnastics as a constructive outlet and a way to relieve the constant stress at home. Gymnastics, and being the last of three children, where I could learn from the mistakes of my older siblings, set me on a much better path than they chose. I will be forever grateful for these blessings.

During high school, after getting my nose broken and not being reset, I started getting sinus infections regularly and having difficulty breathing through my nose due to my deviated septum. When the doctor asked me what happened, I lied and said it was due to being struck in the face with a baseball when I was in the fifth grade. After all, it felt like that was what happened. I played almost every sport as a child, so the doctor easily believed it.

Over time, my sinus infections got worse. By the time I was a senior in high school, my deviated septum had developed nasal polyps, which further limited my nasal capacity to breathe and increased the regularity of my sinus infections. At the end of my senior year, the ear, nose, and throat (ENT) doctor recommended I get surgery to fix my deviated septum (septoplasty). When we told my father that this was the recommended long-term solution, he asked me, "How did you break your nose?"

Did he just ask me how I broke my nose?

RAGE for the man who had beaten me so many times quickly welled up in my body.

A few months prior, I had just won the individual gymnastics state championship, broken the state record in the All Around (all 6 events), and felt strong as an ox—empowered. In this moment, adrenaline and rage were quickly boiling up inside of me as my body was preparing to kick his fucking ass if he did not admit to what he had done to me seven years earlier.

I looked at him squarely in the face and said in a very direct tone, "How the fuck do you not know how I broke my nose?"

He looked at me with confusion, seeing that I was visibly angry, as I had never spoken to or looked at him this way before.

"Don't you remember?" I asked, with my fists clenched. I stared at him with the same stone-cold eyes he had looked at me so many times before, and I said: "Don't you remember, YOU DID IT! When I stepped in front of you when you were chasing (my brother)?"

He paused for a moment to assess what was happening. I remember thinking, *Yeah . . . you better give me the right fucking answer.*

He recognized and quickly adapted to the newfound information and turn of events. He then chuckled to himself a bit and said, "This is why you shouldn't stick your nose into someone else's fight." He paid for the surgery, and we never spoke about the incident again.

What I know now is that when he hit me in the face as a child, he was triggered to black out and didn't really remember. Just like his father had done to him, only this was his version of the unresolved pain repeating their patterns!!

This exchange of words empowered me to stand up to my father and begin to break the authoritarian control he had over me. After this exchange, I started to flex my wings, and his acknowledgment of who I was becoming fueled my independence. Unfortunately, this incident and others like it caused him to recoil in his support for me.

Shortly after this incident, when it came time for me to graduate from high school, he did not like my attitude, so he decided he would not attend the ceremony. His very childish (wounded) part of him thought it best to stay home while I graduated high school, for no other reason than to 'show me.'

This pissed me off and negated the only kind words he'd said to me a few months prior. Just after I won the all-around and broke the state record, I became a state champion. He told me, "I'm proud of you."

I remember hearing those words because when he said them to me, I felt a physical recoil. I remember feeling that those words weren't for me. . . they couldn't be for me because they didn't even closely represent what he had imprinted upon me to this point.

Here I am, his last kid, a state champion who outperformed most in school and sports, and was accepted to the University of Kansas with Honors due to my high ACT scores, yet he didn't care enough to watch me graduate. No wonder we never felt loved by our father. This was the cherry on top, which motivated me to become as self-sufficient as I could and find a way out of his control.

This I Know!

6

FAILING TO MANAGE MY BROTHER'S DYSREGULATION

Family, no matter how hard we try to help each other out, we typically fail because our challenges and dysfunctions are too intertwined.

In the fall of 1988, I enrolled at the University of Kansas (KU) and was accepted into the honors program. At KU, I studied and graduated with a Bachelor of Arts in Human Biology. I didn't graduate with honors because my grades weren't quite high enough for that distinction, due to dealing with a lot of family issues and working my way through much of college to ensure I had enough money to pay for my education. My father (mostly) paid for my room and board, but anything else I had to work for. A couple of semesters, he was pissed off at my "bad attitude," so he withheld tuition support.

His love and care for me were conditional *because his love for himself was conditional.*

I knew I couldn't count on him, so I always kept a few thousand dollars in my bank account from construction work during my summers to be sure I could bridge any financial gaps. I was determined to graduate from college and be able to support myself so I could escape my dependence on a man who created significant disturbances to my consciousness.

In the first two years of college, I lived in a fraternity, and this is how I was introduced to the Marine Corps Officer Selection Officer (OSO). An older fraternity brother, for whom I had a lot of respect, was joining after he graduated. I decided to see what it was all about, and the Marine Corps OSO made his pitch. "We are the best military service, and you probably aren't good enough to be one of us. The Marines are looking for a few hyper-competitive individuals. Don't feel bad that you probably won't make it through the selection process."

Since I had locked in the self-perception and worldview that I was alone and could count only on myself. My view of my young self was inflated, as narcissistic behaviors or beliefs and childhood trauma are intricately linked. I created a narcissistic narrative to support my fragile, young ego as a coping mechanism. I could not count on my parents to keep me safe, so I had to do it. Taking care of myself at such a young age, with a young person's mind, instilled in me an outward sense of self-worth that made me feel bulletproof.

My sense of being bulletproof was also what made me so perfect for the Marine Corps OSO's pitch. Young men, like me, have the attitude that 'I am better than almost everyone around me.' My internal dialogue to myself when I heard the pitch was, *Who the fuck are you to tell me I am not good enough to be one of you?*

They set the bait, and I fell for the lure.

After two six-week training periods at Quantico during the summers between my freshman-sophomore and sophomore-junior years of college, I was hooked and joined the Marine Corps after graduating. To this day, anytime I hear the Marine Corps Hymn, I stand proud and can feel the hairs on the back of my neck stand up.

The last two years of college, I moved back into my childhood home with my drug-addicted brother and three other guys. My parents had moved out of this home, but did not want to sell due to the tax consequences associated with their age. I could live there for free for just under two years, or rent a place somewhere else and pay for it. I chose the "free" option even though it included having to live with my older brother, who, by this point in his life, was struggling with severe mental health and drug addiction issues. He had become as emotionally dysregulated, if not more so, than my father, and his dependence upon drugs and alcohol only reinforced these dysregulations. I was naive enough to think I might be able to help him since I had taken a few psychology courses at KU.

One of my old roommates recently mentioned to me that he locked himself in his bedroom with his dresser pushed up against the bedroom door after witnessing one of the fights between my brother and me. He told me how my brother took a hammer to me. When he told me this, I didn't even remember this incident because routine events like this were not very memorable for me - they were my 'normal'. As you can imagine, events like this made our roommate situation a revolving door. Unfortunately, my brother's addiction and troubles kept spiraling down. My ability to help manage his behavior, while working and going to school, was failing.

He had recently been arrested for pulling out an AR-15 assault rifle that had been converted to fully automatic, and he was awaiting a federal trial for this illegal weapon. He did this because the bartender (rightfully so) refused to serve him any more alcohol due to his level of intoxication that early afternoon. After this incident, he was put on house arrest with an ankle bracelet, so feeding his addiction was difficult, which gave him severe depression. He used his depression to play victim to the medical and religious fields. In this effort, he was able to get prescriptions for painkillers and anxiety.

He, of course, was not taking them appropriately.

After work one day, I go into my brother's bedroom and ask him a question. He answers me in a mushy 'word salad' way, which doesn't make much sense. I ask him the question again. This time, it is a little better, but he slightly slurs his words as he tries to respond to me in a way to mask his level of inebriation. His ability to answer my question is severely impaired, and I quickly see that he is fucked up and not making a ton of sense. Immediately, I am pissed off, so I locate and take the pill bottles from the desk in his room. I tell him, "No more!!"

This, of course, infuriates him. He starts to yell and scream at me about how these are "Doctor-prescribed medicines." I shake my head as I walk out of his bedroom, through the house, and into the garage with his prescriptions. He follows me into the garage as he yells at me to "give him his pills back." On the way out, he grabs an eight-inch chef's knife to confront me with.

By this time, I am two inches taller and about twenty-five pounds heavier than he is, so he always confronts me with some weapon—usually a hammer or a bat, though. I am so used to being hit with some blunt object that by this point, all they do is cause me to come at him quicker and harder. This is probably why he grabbed a knife instead.

In the garage, he points the knife at me as he yells at me to "Give (him his) pills back!"

I let him know that this is not happening because he is obviously fucked up. So, we go back and forth a few verbal rounds, but he isn't having any luck convincing me to give them back. So, in a drugged-up state, he charges at me with the chef's knife. I step back and to the left, deflecting the blade to the right. He stumbles past me, and I quickly get behind him while putting his arms behind him in a 'chicken-wing' maneuver.

"Drop the knife!" I yell.

He screams back, "Give me my pills, or I will stab you!" I don't listen, so he yells at me again, "Give me my pills back!"

Again, I tell him, "Drop the knife!!"

At this point, neither of us is listening to the other. So, with his right hand, he stabs me square on the tip of my hip bone. Immediately, I feel an intense rush of pain and adrenaline as the tip of the blade penetrates my right femur. I throw him face-first into the wall, utilizing the rush of adrenaline that was coursing through my veins. He drops the knife and runs back into the house, into his bedroom, and locks the door.

Mentally, I am a little in shock, like, *What the fuck just happened?*

I want to chase after my brother and give him a serious ass-beating, but instead, I need to attend to the cut as I watch the blood run down my leg. Luckily, because there is no muscle in that area and the skin is very close to the bone, I received only a minor laceration, about a centimeter wide. Even though I am in serious pain, I can easily stop the bleeding, cover the cut with butterfly tape and a Band-Aid, and avoid further medical care, as I had learned that medical care for domestic violence was not an option.

However, the knife had pierced deeply enough into my femur that for the next dozen or so years, I would always feel pain in the head of my femur whenever the weather brought a change in barometric pressure. I would liken it to an 'old man's hip' at the age of twenty. It let me know of the upcoming weather change and reminded me of a previous storm.

This incident taught me that I was woefully ill-equipped to help my brother in his mental health battle and that I had to let him go if I were to continue my path in life. A few hours after the incident, I had to take a college final exam. I had a B-minus going into the final, but because of the day's activities, I couldn't concentrate or remember much, so I bombed the final. . . *badly*. I went from a B-minus to a D-plus in this class. I remember getting my test back and looking at my answers, thinking, *how did I not know that, and why did I answer the questions this way?* I remember verbally berating myself for doing so poorly on this final. In fact, years later, I was still upset at myself for my poor performance and how it negatively affected my grades and GPA.

I now understand that the reason I did so poorly was not due to a lack of studying or preparation, but due to trauma. The inability to concentrate and to recall information after a traumatic event is real!

With my newfound understanding of how traumatic events can affect the mind, I now understand why my brother couldn't remember his multiplication tables and struggled to learn in school after seeing me being whipped with The Belt so many times early in our youth. For me, when I was in college, I had the advantage of a brain that was much more developed, yet I still wasn't equipped to pivot my mind that quickly.

Throughout my college career, family dysfunction and having to work to support myself took my attention away from school, which caused my grades to suffer. Even though I did not graduate with honors, I feel very blessed to be part of the program. In fact, I took many honors psychology courses, which gave me insight into my own personal and family dysfunctions. These courses also provided me with some cognitive tools to better process what I remembered of my dysfunctional childhood, and for this, I will always be grateful!

In fact, one of my very earliest journaling exercises was a letter I wrote to myself while taking a child psychology course at KU. I found the letter inside the textbook many years later. The letter stated all the things I was not going to do to my kids, such as spanking them in anger/rage, or verbally berating or belittling them for the tiniest of mistakes. It also contained the things I was absolutely going to do to them, including telling them I love them, hugging them, and showing them that my love was unconditional. When I found the letter, a dozen or so years after I wrote it, I showed it to my wife. She read it and agreed that I had kept to my word, with maybe a rare exception. This is the power of journaling and the power of making promises to yourself. I unfortunately threw the book away a few years back and forgot the letter was inside. I would love to still have it as a memento.

7

MILITARY CAREER

The Few, The Proud, the Marines: The currency we trade in is human life: First to Fight, First to Die! Because of the high stakes, it can be a chronically stressful career.

For many, the military is a brotherhood and sisterhood—the family they never had. The Marines were the best family I had ever known when I joined, and I love the brothers and sisters with whom I served. Military service can be a very rewarding career. I know I loved my career—and I have no regrets about my twenty-one years as an active-duty Marine. My military service made me a better man than I would have been if I had stayed in Lawrence, KS, and worked for my father. I saw the world, met new people, and encountered new ideas. All of which opened my mind to new ways of thinking and living.

The Marine Corps is affectionately known as Uncle Sam's Misguided Children (U.S.M.C.). I think the nickname is appropriate. To survive or thrive in the Marine Corps, you must be better than the main pack. You must be able to withstand more pain and challenges than any other regular military forces or most civilians. After all, we are 'The First to Fight.' This is not to diminish the value of the other branches of service or civilian life. This is what my experience has taught me, and it helps to explain why we are the way we are. Our nickname is 'Devil Dog,' which the Germans gave us at Belleau Woods during World War I. They gave us this nickname because we fight like Devil Dogs. We never give up and continue to fight to our last breath. We do this out of love for our fellow Marines. If I can die and save another, then my effort will be worth it. I know this is the same attitude many of the people I served with had.

In boot camp or Officer Candidate School (OCS), the Marine Corps strips you of your individuality so you can assimilate into the Marine Corps ethos and put mission over individual comfort. The Marine Corps simultaneously builds you up to feel bulletproof, all while stripping away selfish behaviors. In other words, the Marine Corps knows that during your career, you will be exposed to some extremely significant physical and mental challenges and quite possibly traumatic ones as well. The Marine Corps wants only those who can handle extreme stress to wear its uniform, so much of its indoctrination training is designed to see if you crack under pressure; if you do, you are removed before you ever wear the uniform.

When I joined the Marine Corps, fewer than one-half of the officer candidates completed training and became Marine officers. Those who have already been routinely challenged through sports, suffered abuse, or grown up in challenging environments, find it much easier to adapt to the Marine Corps than those who entered from homes where they grew up in a relatively stress-free environment, or their helicopter parents coddled them and never had to face adversity. In other words, I was a very good fit.

Every young Marine officer attends The Basic School (TBS) in Quantico for six months. This is a very important aspect of the 'Rite of Passage' to being a Marine leader. This is where each young officer learns a little about all the military jobs and is given a *perspective* on what each job does and its needs and concerns to support the warfighting effort. TBS was instrumental in my growth because it gave me perspective on what it meant to be a cog in the wheel of a warfighting machine and how every cog needs to do their job and work with each other. *Perspective* provides understanding, understanding provides *compassion for others,* and is a building block for the 'Esprit de Corps' or camaraderie that the

Marine Corps is famous for. We are the only U.S. military service that brings all of its new officers to the same school and forces these young officers to do each other's jobs for six months so that each and every Marine officer gets a feel for what it takes to be in the other person's boots. This comes at great cost to the taxpayer, but it saves lives and wins battles. The ability to view a problem from various perspectives has served me extremely well throughout my life and is a key theme throughout this book.

This I Know!

8

EMOTIONAL INTELLIGENCE AND HOVERING A HELICOPTER

There is no separation of knowledge and emotions. We store emotions in our subconscious along with our knowledge. The past should be a place of reference, not a place of residence. The past is a place of learning, not a place of living. Piloting our emotions comes from the past and from where our triggers and emotional outbursts manifest.

After six months of basic training at TBS, I was sent down to Pensacola, Florida, for flight training. During my flight training in the T-34C aircraft, I quickly realized that I was not equipped to fly jets. During the Precision Aerobatics section of flight training, my body did not respond well to the higher G loads. In fact, these maneuvers gave me migraine headaches, which exhausted me physically. I chose helicopters because I felt that flying should feel like a reward, not a punishment.

As I began my helicopter flight training, one of the first things they taught me was to hover the helicopter. Learning to hover a helicopter is one of the most unnatural skills I have had to learn. You are continuously moving your right arm in some pattern within a circle, while moving your left arm up and down, while also moving your feet back and forth and in opposite directions—all in an effort to go nowhere. I won't even mention all the buttons, sliders, and toggle switches on those hand grips.

Learning to hover a helicopter at flight school takes several flights. This skill is a gradual development of muscle memory to the point where it can be performed without conscious thought.

First, the instructor gives you only the cyclic (right-hand) stick. This stick controls the overhead blades (rotors). They operate like a fan blowing down. The stick controls the direction of the overhead fan, so if the helicopter starts moving left, you need to move the stick to the right so the fan tilts to push more air to the left. This input stops you from moving left, but if you do not take the input out at the right time, you will start to drift right. You need to take the input out at the proper time. Lastly, you need to find a spot in the middle that keeps you stable in one location. To stop drifting in any direction requires three inputs: one to counter, one to stop, and one to stabilize. This creates a constant need to make small but meaningful adjustments to keep the helicopter from moving forward, backward, left, or right. Doing this requires significant brainpower because one is *consciously* thinking about what is happening and what to do to stop the motion.

The first time a student is given this task, they can do it for a few seconds, but then start to lose control because their inputs are either too large or too small. They haven't learned how the aircraft responds to the input they are providing. So, the instructor will take the controls and show the student how much input represents how much reaction. The student is given each controller individually until they develop enough muscle memory to perform the task more naturally or with less conscious effort. Eventually, the student is given all the controllers at once and must control all three [cyclic (right-hand stick), collective (left-hand stick) & pedals] in coordination with each other and perform each motion with little to no *conscious thought*.

Learning to hover a helicopter is so mentally tiring because, initially, *everything is done consciously.* Conscious effort requires much more brain power and energy than subconscious effort. While you can pick up hovering a helicopter in a few hours spread over a week or two, it takes months to be able to hover while talking on the radio or engaging in other activities. You have to develop enough muscle memory that your brain can take in the external environmental cues, process the information, and do the actions without *consciously* thinking about what you are doing. In other words, pilots need to be able to fly or hover the helicopter from their *subconscious mind,* freeing up the conscious mind for other endeavors.

Emotional intelligence is very similar and begins to develop at a very young age. In fact, as babies, we are not emotionally regulated at all because being cared for or fed can be a life-or-death situation since babies are unable to care for themselves. Thus, every meal feels like it could be their last should a caregiver not respond to their immediate needs. It is through being fed on time that babies learn they are seen and their needs are heard, so they can begin to self-soothe or dampen their emotional responses.

As adults, much of how we perceive or respond to the world is held in our subconscious mind, which is based on earlier experiences with other human beings and on past experiences when we were in a much more vulnerable or fearful state.

In my effort to explore the science behind my healing, I have learned that our autonomic nervous system regulates our emotions. Autonomic, meaning we do not control them, but they control us. This autonomic nervous system is like a dial that puts our body into either a heightened state of awareness or relaxes or downregulates its ability to respond to the environment or a threat.

In simple terms, they are two sides of the same dial, with a rheostat that lets you dial up one side, but when you do . . . you dial down the other side. In other words, the more you activate the sympathetic side of the dial, the less active the parasympathetic side is.

The sympathetic nervous system is the part of your nervous system that carries signals related to your "fight-or-flight" response. When the sympathetic nervous system is activated, it speeds up your heart rate, delivers more blood to areas of your body that need more oxygen, and triggers other responses to help you get out of danger. This response, when fully activated (in panic), also shuts down higher cognitive brain functions. After all, one does not need to perform complex math problems while trying to run from a lion. In this effort, the hypothalamus in the brain acts as the conductor, releasing neurotransmitter chemicals into your bloodstream to prep the brain and body for action. We commonly refer to these chemicals (norepinephrine, epinephrine, and acetylcholine) as 'adrenaline.'

On the opposite side of the dial is the parasympathetic nervous system. Your parasympathetic nervous system relaxes your body after periods of stress or danger. It also helps run life-sustaining processes, such as digestion, healing, and learning, during times when you feel safe and relaxed. This relaxed state allows other parts of the brain to be active, including those responsible for learning or critical thinking.

The problem arises when a child's or a person's chronic environment is one of danger or stress. This regularly shifts the autonomic nervous system toward the sympathetic side, moving the baseline or resting state from a balanced nervous system to one that favors the sympathetic side. The greater or more persistent the perceived threat, the more the dial is turned toward the sympathetic.

A great tool for examining where you fall on this spectrum is Heart Rate Variability (HRV). A higher HRV indicates a lower-stressed autonomic nervous system. The HRV is the variation in time between consecutive heartbeats. The longer the interval between the heartbeats, the more the autonomic nervous system is tilted toward the parasympathetic or 'rest and digest' side. The lower the HRV score, the more the nervous system is tilted toward the sympathetic, fight-or-flight side. If you find your resting HRV to be low, you would benefit from a regular practice of the *physiological sigh* (two short inhales followed by one long and deep exhale) or other intentional breathwork patterns where you exhale at half the rate of inhale. These techniques have an immediate calming effect on your nervous system. Breathwork is our primary tool for managing our physiological response to stress.

My brother responded classically to our chronically stressful environment. The chronic stress of home life and his strong sympathetic response (panic) to traumatic events turned off the parts of his brain that controlled his higher cognitive thinking. This 'normal' response severely limited his ability to learn as a child, which affected him into adulthood.

Emotional intelligence is directly tied to the autonomic nervous system. Piloting one's emotions can be like a person trying to hover a helicopter. Depending on the external environment, hovering a helicopter can be easy if the conditions are stable, or very difficult if there are strong gusts constantly blowing you around.

If a child is raised in a dysfunctional environment, where they do not feel safe, it can make it extremely difficult to 'learn to hover' their emotional behavior. As I mentioned before, we are born without emotional regulation due to the immediate and constant care we require for survival as infants. As babies learn from their environment, they learn to soothe or tone down their emotional responses when the environment tends to their needs quickly and appropriately. If a baby is hungry, he begins to cry, and the longer the baby is without food, the longer and harder he will cry. Imagine an adult crying as soon as they get a little hungry. It would seem very inappropriate because a little hunger as an adult will not kill you, but as a baby, you have not learned when being hungry is a life-or-death situation . . . or not.

In fact, our human emotions are designed and built to strongly react from the start. We are wired to overreact from the start. So, if you find yourself overeating, this is a strong clue you have unresolved dis-ease from your past. This is how emotional intelligence is built. Our emotional regulation is built from repeated, stable, and trusted responses from our caregivers that teach the baby and young child to soothe (downregulate) these strong emotions and reactions. In other words, babies and young children need a stable environment to feel safe enough to tune down their default emotional responses (crying, temper tantrums, etc.). When you see a child overreact, the best thing you can do is not match their energy but do your best to bring them down to a more stable, regulated state.

As babies turn into toddlers, which turn into adolescent children. If the environment has not been stable enough for long enough, the child has not learned to regulate their emotional responses well enough for their age, as is considered 'normal.' This lack of emotional regulation, as seen through child development models, manifests as 'abnormal' child psychology and behavior for the child's age. I witnessed classical 'abnormal' behavior in not only my father but also both of my siblings, as I am sure they did in me.

I witnessed the trouble my older siblings had with their emotional regulation due to the chaotic and turbulent environment we were all in. The stormy environment under which we were learning to hover our emotions caused all of us, at times, to overcorrect/overreact. Similar to a young pilot putting in too much stick movement to counter a helicopter's drift.

We do not teach beginner pilots to hover or fly during stormy weather with strong or gusty winds because we know this only serves to introduce bad habits or improper actions under 'normal' weather conditions. Unfortunately, many children, myself included, are required to learn in unstable environments as they learn to 'pilot' their emotions.

For those of us who learned to 'hover' our emotions under duress, it can be difficult to respond appropriately to minor altercations. We build in emotional triggers that cause an over-reaction (hypervigilance or panic) or under-correction (disassociation, numbness) to the perceived environment due to experiences in the past during which the child was not properly cared for.

Emotional intelligence begins at a very young age, and I do not think humanity understands or honors this aspect of the human experience very well. Dr. Gabor Mate discusses how the bio-psycho-social environment that many of us are born into creates a toxic environment that prevents humans from properly developing.

The book *The Boy Who Was Raised as a Dog* by Dr. Bruce Perry does an excellent job of describing how trauma and neglect affect the young mind and how a child can get extremely dysregulated at such a young age, should they lack appropriate care when exposed to traumatic events. I know this to be true as I witnessed my father's actions and my brother's reactions (and my sisters to a much lesser extent). A young mind is extremely powerful yet vulnerable at the same time, because our greatest unprocessed learning occurs between birth and age 5.

During our first five or so years, we take our experiences in and accept them at face value. This sets the baseline programming for our emotional behavior or default mode network. This is how our emotional default mode network is developed. For those who grew up in a very dysfunctional or traumatic environment, this network can remain dysregulated to a point that the child cannot seem to behave 'normally' for their age. If actions are not taken to address the previous distress without resolution, these 'abnormal' behaviors can extend into adulthood as they did for my father and brother, and to a much lesser extent . . . in me.

To unwind or reprogram your default behaviors or responses to earlier distress, you have to go back to the original distress and resolve it to remove the underlying activation or dysregulation. Dr. Perry does an excellent job explaining how therapists approach treatment for some of the most traumatized children.

Later in life, my dad stated that my brother seemed 'off' or 'challenged' from a young age. I believe that it was the constant fear, abuse, and unresolved disturbances in my brother's state of consciousness at a very young age that led to his severe dysregulation. He eventually was diagnosed as having bipolar disorder (BPD) due to the emotional swings in his behavior. Looking back through the lens of trauma, it now appears that his mood swings were directly related to developmental problems related to his early traumatic events and living in fear.

My brother's nervous system never became balanced because it was always on alert, and his baseline shifted toward the sympathetic side. This limited my brother's ability to 'rest and digest' what he just did or learned. 'Rest, digest, and learning' can only happen when the child or person is in a relaxed or calm state and a place of safety.

When a child has not had a stable, nurturing environment, their nervous system fails to downregulate the sympathetic response. I witnessed my brother act out and behave badly, and not be able to properly respond to their environment or think clearly, due to this developmental psychological manifestation. This is not because he was bad or stupid, but because the environment did not nurture him enough for his system to learn to trust that he would be properly cared for.

Should you see children or adults around you acting like disturbed children, instead of asking, "What is wrong with you?" one should ask, "What happened to you?" as the book with the same title explores. Be *curious* about this behavior rather than judging it. Understand they are emotionally dysregulated to the point they cannot behave normally. The best thing you can do for them is to try to help them get back to a regulated emotional and mental state.

My brother struggled to learn because he was scared most days my father was around. My brother was a sensitive child who desperately wanted his dad's attention and love. He was an emotionally sensitive child who stayed in the chaotic energy my father carried. Therefore, he spent much more time around my father, which put him in a more chronically stressful environment than I did. Because he spent much more time around my father and was scared about how my father would respond, his ability to rest, digest, or learn was turned down or off much of the time. His brain was busy reading the room and preparing to respond quickly to any potential threat. My brother did not have the gift of dissociation; therefore, it dramatically hindered his ability to develop the parts of the brain that allow for critical thinking (the prefrontal cortex).

I know that when my dad came home, everyone was on alert. What was his mood? How was Mom acting? My siblings chose to stay in this chaotic environment and try to navigate it, whereas I would immediately go to my room, where the environment was more stable. I would wait for a significant period and only venture out when the environment was calm and stable for a considerable period. This greatly helped reduce the chaotic environment I experienced. This is where my brother and I diverged in our response to this shared chronic stress and traumatic home environment.

Because I was deeply afraid of my father, I would retreat to my room anytime he was around. I would avoid my father so I could exist in a less chaotic environment. I chose not to read the room but to avoid the situation altogether.

My severe beatings taught me to stay away. Additionally, I was blessed with the ability to disassociate from my emotions when my stress rose high enough. It was like a circuit breaker that kicked in and kept me from panicking and limited my sympathetic response. By dissociating from my feelings, which kept me from panicking, I was able to use the rush of adrenaline to feed all parts of my brain. Thus, I was able to assess and react to the situation with an active mind. This provided me the ability to better learn from my deeply traumatic experiences. Therefore, I am deeply grateful for this blessing!

As an adult, I have had a few people question me on how I was able to do so well, considering everything they knew about our deeply dysfunctional home life. They could see how negatively it had affected my older siblings' behaviors. I never had a satisfying answer until now.

My childhood did not deeply affect me, like it did my older siblings, because I hid from the abuse the best I could. Additionally, when it was my turn in the 'hot seat' of abuse, I disassociated from it and never processed much of it either. Instead, I packed the memories away and hid these events and the associated feelings even from myself until I was fifty-four years old.

This coping mechanism of avoidance and disassociation, over time, built up subconscious anxiety and distress, which prevented me from moving forward and through my stress. It built up over a lifetime and prevented my happiness and negatively affected my mental health. Too many events of my life and their associated emotions sat repressed and unresolved. Eventually, they built up to the point I was disassociating from life daily because my voice of beratement was so prevalent and pronounced. This angry voice was severing my connection to the world, and, if I am being truthful, it was also closing me off from myself.

The earlier one has significant wind gusts (traumatic event or crisis of safety or support), the greater the social-emotional development can be affected. Now that I have been able to recall and properly process those repressed memories from my early youth, I have found that my emotional intelligence has improved significantly. I had to love my 'child self' and fully accept what happened to him. By removing the disturbances in my subconscious that had resided for forty plus years, I was able to become a mentally healthier and happier individual.

I was able to reset my emotional intelligence and my ability to properly respond through deep self-reflection, inner work, and examining my life through the lens of trauma. For me, to get to and process those disassociated memories, I utilized psychedelic medicine. You may not need this powerful a tool; in fact, I hope you do not. By looking inward to my past with the aid of psychedelic medicine, I was able to recover traumatic memories and resolve repressed subconscious emotional activations. I was able to remove the disturbances in my subconscious that got locked away as a small child and had been affecting me my entire life . . . until now.

It is the neuroplasticity these medicines provide, under therapeutic conditions, that creates the conditions for rewriting our subconscious emotional activations from our past. These medicines, under the right 'set and setting', allow reprogramming to occur. Now that my autonomic nervous system and default mode network are more relaxed, I can easily handle difficult emotional situations that previously caused me significant struggle to avoid overreacting. Think "white knuckling" or repressing significant emotional thoughts or feelings.

If you find yourself having to "white knuckle" through a situation or feel an overwhelming urge to run, or you shift into severe anxiety or anger, I highly recommend that you get to the bottom of where these emotional responses manifest from originally. Trained therapists can help you uncover where these behaviors manifest from. A great question to ask yourself is, "When did I first feel this way?" This helps to lead you to the initial distress without resolution. If you can find and resolve the original distress, you can remove its subconscious activation. If anything resonates with you, please go back and look into your past. It is only through going back and revisiting old wounds that you can remove their emotional imprinting and subconscious activations. You are worth it, and your life will be happier for it.

Life is so much easier when you are not struggling to hold it together. There are many tools at one's disposal for regulating one's emotions. Simple breathwork, exercise, or listening to soothing or positive music can do the trick. Other times, it takes talk therapy or journaling to find meaning or understand what is happening in our lives. Trained therapists, psychologists, or psychiatrists can help resolve many of our disturbances with the tools they are trained in (EMDR, somatic techniques, etc.).

For those who have significant or early disturbances, psychedelic medicine, under the right set and setting, and guidance, can have profound healing effects that are more effective than traditional methods. With proper guidance, these powerful medicines can help you to access and turn off the emotional dysregulations held in your subconscious, which activate your autonomic nervous system as they did for me. This requires not only the proper set, setting, and intention but also post-consumption integration, which may take several weeks, months, or even years to fully understand and incorporate.

As I write this, I am over two years into my integration and still learning! With these powerful medicines, you can begin to see your experiences with a newfound *perspective*. It is the new perspective that facilitates the release of the emotional distress that accompanied the original experience. In other words, these powerful medicines can be the tool to release what no longer serves you and to rewrite the neural pathways in your brain that affect you.

Now that I have removed many of my subconscious disturbances, I can respond to the present appropriately and not react from a place in the past. I now respond instinctively and with much less emotional baggage from my past.

My emotional intelligence is so much better because it has been repaired at the subconscious, neural, or DNA level (epigenetic expression). In other words, I can now subconsciously hover my emotions, even when life is stormy. I may get a little dysregulated or blown around, but to a much lesser extent. After the event is over, I can return to a stable hover or an emotionally regulated mindset much more quickly.

This being said, as an adult, because the grooves of this neural response went on for so long, I still unwittingly use my trauma responses when people get emotionally activated around me. I emotionally and physically retreat to a space that feels safe for me- avoidant personality trait. On one side, it allows me to assess the situation with a clear mind and limit my own emotional dysregulation, on the other side, my emotional retreat can feel like emotional abandonment to the people I love which only exacerbates the present situation. Integration is not only being aware, but being mindful enough to be able to change these old patterns when you see yourself falling into them.

Prior to my transformation, I also routinely carried similar emotional dysregulation energy that my father had, although a much toned-down version than what my father brought.

What we don't resolve, we repeat in our own way!!

My wife has recently stated that she had to read my emotional energy to feel emotionally safe, especially since returning from war the first time. My emotional dysregulation caused her dysregulation, which led to her excess alcohol consumption, and thus, our generational trauma cycle continued.

Remember, we store emotions along with the memories that difficult experiences imprint on us. We have to resolve the associated feelings of the original distress to eliminate their subconscious activations. They are inseparable until we resolve the original distress.

This I Know!

9

INCLEMENT WEATHER AND DEPRESSION

Both reduce your ability to see, understand, and navigate your environment.

Fast forward a few years: I finished flight school, selected the AH-1W Cobra Attack Helicopter as my aviation platform, moved to Camp Pendleton for training, got married, and then moved to Jacksonville, North Carolina, where I joined my first tactical squadron.

All Naval aircraft have a 'bible' called NATOPS, or Naval Aviation Training and Operating Procedures Standardization manual. The manual contains information on all systems (electrical, hydraulic, and engine) and procedures for addressing system failures (emergency procedures, or EPs). This manual contains all previous lessons learned on how to deal with failures in any aspect of the aircraft. We, military pilots, say that "the emergency procedures are written in blood," meaning that some people died because they took the wrong action, at the wrong time, or in the wrong order. We beat the emergency procedures into our young pilots' brains and run them through practice failures to instill knowledge and develop 'muscle memory' as a means for their survival. We do this so that if the pilot panics and cannot think, then they can still do the actions from their subconscious memory. One of the key elements that we indoctrinate our young military pilots with is the mantra "Aviate, Navigate, Communicate." This mantra becomes their default setting should they become overwhelmed.

Aviate means to fly the aircraft, first and foremost. If you can't do anything else, keep the aircraft flying.

Navigate means pointing the aircraft in a safe direction and, if you know where you are and where you need to go, flying your route.

Communicate who you are and what you are doing. This is the least important task, so it is the first thing you stop doing when you are being mentally overwhelmed.

Aviate, Navigate, Communicate is ingrained in every pilot as the core operating mode. We do this because we, military pilots, are required to fly into dangerous environments such as bad weather, or with degraded aircraft systems (engine or hydraulic failure . . .), or combat. This mantra helps pilots survive.

Pilots memorize this survival mantra as the Aviator's 'Default Mode Network,' which provides a fallback position should the pilot become overwhelmed and begin to lose the ability to think or remain fully in control. This mantra reminds the pilot to task shed and only do what one is capable of at the time and in the order of importance. One of my earliest tests that required me to rely on this wisdom occurred during my first deployment on an amphibious aircraft carrier (USS *Saipan* LHA-2), when we were conducting flying operations in the Mediterranean Sea off the southwest coast of Sardinia.

On the night of October 13th, 1998, I was a young Captain flying the final mission on the final day of a combined military operation with our Spanish and Italian partners. Due to the inclement weather of the previous days, we had extra ordnance (bullets, rockets, and bombs) to expend to achieve our training objectives.

I was the lead aircraft and served as the airborne Forward Air Controller (FAC), directing battle operations. I was in control of all the aircraft (AH-1W's, F-18's, Harriers), as well as the artillery (155mm Howitzers), and naval guns (Spanish frigate *Andalucia*-F72). I coordinated when and where each platform delivered its weapons. There were VIPs in attendance this night, and we wanted the VIP spectators on the observation hill to see 'the show.' It was extremely dark out due to an overcast sky with pockets of rain, so I utilized the artillery to provide coordinated illumination of the battle area so everyone could see the mission. We had several aircraft lined up at various contact points with full weapons loads, and the Spanish frigate was sailing offshore with (20) -five-inch diameter bullets for this mission. I gave each platform its mission tasking by radio via a Nine-Line brief or Call for Fire instructions.

Because this was a training mission with live weapons, my instructions and timing were being monitored and double-checked to ensure safety, which slowed down the process. Additionally, inclement weather caused a delay. We had the fixed-wing aircraft deliver their bombs first; next came the helicopters delivering our rockets and guns. All of this took place while we had artillery illuminate the target area just in front of the observers, but out of the way of aircraft traffic.

Due to an internal issue with the Spanish naval guns, there was a delay in their portion. This required me to send my wingman back to the ship early due to his fuel concerns. After the destroyer finished its last rounds 'in effect,' I checked off station and headed back to the expected location of the ship.

We were short on fuel, but had enough based on our understanding of where the ship was expected to be. As we head back out to sea and check in with the ship on the radios, we learn the ship is several miles farther out than planned, putting us in a critical fuel situation.

As I looked down at my fuel gauge, I did some quick math in my head, and it was apparent we should have just enough fuel to land on the aircraft carrier safely, but just barely. We informed the ship of our low fuel state and coordinated for it to turn toward us so we could be confident we had enough fuel to land.

As we were flying toward the ship, the weather was getting darker with a wall of thunderstorms between us and the ship. In other words, we were flying into a bumpy black hole with almost no visual reference to the horizon. On the way back, when we were about 13 miles from the ship, my instructor pilot (a fellow, but senior Captain) in the rear seat started to get vertigo. He lets me know so I can help monitor his ability to fly the aircraft, be prepared, and talk him through any errors in flight should this be necessary.

I could tell he had 'the leans to the right,' because he kept wanting to drop the right wing below the horizon. I would let him know, and on occasion, I had to bump the stick to level the aircraft. He was having trouble maintaining altitude (1,000 feet above the water) and kept drifting to the right of the course line and descending below the planned altitude.

As the weather was degrading around us, my mind was drawn to an accident that occurred just over a year prior, where a couple of our squadron pilots lost their lives. They died due to getting vertigo while returning to a ship in degraded weather conditions very similar to what we were beginning to face.

One of the pilots who lost their life was a pilot whom I had followed in his footsteps: Captain Bogart. God rest his soul. Every time he moved on from a job, I would be assigned his old job—literally every job. We would joke that I was the new Captain Bogart. I was well aware that vertigo was a contributing factor to what caused him to die, and I now found myself entering into a very similar situation. I remember thinking, *I hope it is not my destiny to continue to follow him this way as well.*

As we approached the aircraft carrier, my fellow Captain's vertigo was interfering with his ability to communicate, so I took over communications with the ship. This is part of crew coordination called task shedding and task sharing. His job was to fly the aircraft (aviate and navigate), and my job was to talk to the ship (communicate). His world was closing in on him, and he was losing the mental resources to handle extraneous tasks. In other words, he was consciously having to fly the aircraft because the conditions had degraded to the point his unconscious 'muscle memory' was overwhelmed.

When we got to about 9 or 10 miles from the ship, the weather had degraded to the point that we no longer had outside visual references, so we requested a Precision Approach Radar (PAR) and asked to transition to Instrument Flight Rules (IFR). We did this so we could be under the direct control of an Air Traffic Controller (ATC) and return safely to the ship. My fellow pilot did not make this transition to instrument flying very well, as it exacerbated his vertigo. His vertigo was now being accompanied by nausea, and he was losing his ability to fly. I had to take over the controls and fly the aircraft back to the ship from the front seat.

As I am flying the aircraft in the dark, bumpy hole, I am getting a first-hand introduction as to why this aircraft was not certified by the FAA to fly in the clouds from the front seat. The FAA refused to certify this aircraft because the main instrument for flying in the clouds (the attitude gyro) was visually obscured by our weapons optical-sight telescoping tube. If the pilot was sitting normally, this cockpit configuration meant the pilot in the front seat had to tilt their head to the right to see the attitude gyro, or lean to the right to see it. Both of those techniques can be vertigo-inducing due to the 'seat of your pants' feeling, which makes you feel as though you are in a turn even when 'wings level.' Both of those techniques can be very disorienting, separating what you are doing from what you are feeling. Since the aircraft was not certified to fly IFR from the front seat, it was to be done only in an emergency, and here I was doing just that. In other words, the situation was getting serious!!

So here I am, flying from the front seat of the aircraft on a dark night in a heavy storm, knowing that my brain and body will send me inaccurate signals. I tell myself, "Believe the gauges (flight instruments)," because I know they're more reliable than I will be in this situation. As I try different head and seat positions to see the attitude gyro. I start to feel a little vertigo and understand why flying instruments from the front seat of an AH-1W in a pitch-black, bouncy thunderstorm is not allowed except in an emergency. As my vertigo is rising sharply and my fellow pilot is mostly incapacitated from his, our options to remain safe are quickly disappearing.

As we are getting closer and being bounced around, lightning is flashing all around us as we enter a storm cell. Hail begins to rapidly and loudly strike the canopy:

Tik.

Tik . . . tik.

Tik . . . tik . . . tik.

This made it extremely difficult to hear the Air Traffic Controller as he gave us flight instructions. I turn up my radio so I can try to make sense of what instructions we are being told to follow. The air traffic controller tells us to turn 80 degrees to the left so we can intercept the final approach radial, which sets us up behind the ship. This large turn triggers vertigo, making my internal compass spin even though the aircraft's gauges showed we were upright and 'wings level.' I keep repeating to myself, *Believe the gauges! Believe the Gauges!*

As the air traffic controller gives us instructions and brings us down the glideslope toward the ship, we are bouncing around pretty aggressively, while hail is rapidly striking the canopy, exacerbating my disorientation. My concern for our safety is causing nausea to rise in my stomach. The 'pucker factor' is rapidly rising as a cauldron of nauseous pain is brewing in my stomach. I squeeze my stomach as I try to prevent the knot in my stomach from overtaking me.

The air traffic controller tells us we are over the ship's stern and to proceed visually. I take my eyes off the flight instruments and peer through my night vision goggles, but all I see is green darkness. I can't see the ship's control tower, which is no more than two hundred feet in front of me. I have a moment of panic, and in that moment . . . time seems to stop. After the eternity of a second or two, I realize that I have no visual reference to the ship with not enough fuel to go around and try again. I am in complete darkness with no way out. This might be the end, I think, as the pain in my stomach turns to a rapid boil and an intense urge to vomit wells up in the pit of my stomach.

I tightly squeeze my stomach so that I do not purge all over the flight gauges in front of me. I suddenly see a light—then two—then four. Before I can make sense of what these dim dots represent, my fellow Captain asks for the controls as he is able to find meaning in the few points of light we see, and he lands us safely on the ship. When the skids touched down on the deck of the ship, the intense nausea roiling in the pit of my stomach relaxed, and a rush of gratitude flooded my brain. I am so very grateful to be alive!!

After my fellow Captain and I landed on the rain-soaked deck, we went below deck and walked through the operations area. Several people are congratulating us on such a successful mission. Since it was the last mission, the mission was played over various common audio channels throughout the ship. Everyone is super motivated, excited, and proud of what our team just accomplished under such difficult conditions.

After paperwork and debriefing, I try to sleep, but I can't. I feel alert, my mind and body buzzing with energy as I try to untangle and unwind a giant mix of emotions swirling inside me. Since I am having no luck settling down, I get out of bed and climb to the top of the ship, and on top of the bridge, and out into the weather.

By now, the storm has passed, and the cool wind feels soothing to my face. As I stand alone in the night, I can see the horizon and stars are peeking out from behind the clouds. What a crazy, strange night, I think. My emotions are swirling as I feel extremely happy and proud of what we just accomplished. At the same time, there was a part of me that was terrified and awestruck by my close brush with death. These emotions, thoughts, and feelings are swirling inside of me like the intense storm cell I just left . . . then, as the sun's first light begins to peer above the horizon.

As I see the light of the new day begin, my love for my family wells up and overtakes me for one of the only times in my adult life. For some reason, I don't or can't repress my emotions. I break down into tears for one of the only times in my adult life. I started to cry for my wife and daughter, and if my son were born, I would have cried for him, too. I have so many emotions swirling through me that I completely lose control. I cry, and I cry hard. On one hand, I am heartbroken that I had almost left my family alone without a chance to say goodbye. On the other hand, I am crying tears of joy for myself and how thankful and grateful I am to be alive. I thank God for allowing me the privilege of continuing to live.

This difficult flight mirrors many people's experiences with depression. The world starts getting darker, and you start not knowing where you are going, or even where you are, or where you fit into this world, or what you have to offer it. The ability or desire to communicate your struggles to others becomes too difficult, or you are met with indifference.

In the months following my mother's death, my father was having significant difficulty understanding his place in the world, as he had lost all his desire to work and was struggling to understand the meaning of my mother's death and my brother's drug addiction. He would tell me he felt like a failure in so many ways. He blamed himself for their struggles. He wasn't wrong, but I did my best to put his mind at ease, even though my mind was having similar thoughts.

He told me in a letter to me only a few weeks before his suicide that "the light was beginning to flicker" and that he was "learning to trust in a higher power" when he felt his "own power was inadequate." I took this as a sign that he was getting better and that I didn't need to worry or call him as much . . . so I didn't. Unfortunately, he extinguished his light for good when the repressed emotions and his pain became too great for him to understand their meaning and teachings. For many years since his death, I have beaten myself up for not being there for him when he needed me at the end.

For those who have loved ones who suffer from severe depression or have committed suicide, I offer that *we only know what we know when we know it*. Because of the darkness and storm clouds that surrounded him, he didn't know that life could have—would have—gotten better if he had allowed himself the grace to accept and process the storm that resided inside his head. Contained in that flickering light that he was beginning to see was *compassion* and *forgiveness*. The darkness of storms comes and always passes if we can believe the gauges that a higher power provides us and hold on long enough to get through them.

Looking back, this flight never left me with any negative emotions. If anything, this flight, which I now have in my toolbox, helped to lift me up and provide me the *courage* to face future great unknowns for my safety. I now understand that the reason it empowered me was that I allowed myself to cry and release, to purge the negative energy rather than hold onto the fear and sadness. This traumatic event did not become trauma because I released and purged through crying. Crying can be that powerful! I would not fully understand the importance of crying until I went to Costa Rica and met the purgative power of ayahuasca, which I will discuss later.

I also see this flight as a moment that strengthened my steel, gave me more resolve and confidence for future flights . . . combat flights!

This I Know!

10

STRENGTHENING THE STEEL

Appropriate heat and pressure make steel stronger. The same can be said of the human mind. Stress creates opportunity for growing and learning. It takes mindfulness, understanding, and compassion to make the most of life's toughest moments.

In the summer of 2002, I was assigned to teach students how to investigate aircraft crashes at the School of Aviation Safety located in Monterey, California. Prior to teaching my class on material failure, I would show the 1986 Marine Corps commercial where they take raw steel, heat it, apply intense pressure, and polish it until it becomes a Marine Corps sword. In the end, the raw steel is a beautiful sword: shiny, strong, and deadly. This is a great visualization of how Marines are made. I used it as an intro to discuss how materials are strengthened . . . or how they can be weakened or fail.

This process of strengthening steel is called forging. A very simple explanation of forging a steel sword: Intense pressure is applied to the heated steel with a heavy hammer. This beating puts intense pressure on the metal, causing it to soften and remove voids, pockets, and other defects. The sword is then returned to the fire so that the newly aligned material can rejoin and reform into a stronger configuration. The heat provides the conditions for the material to reform in the newly configured and aligned state. If done properly, forging strengthens the material. Conversely, if these two processes are not performed in the correct amounts or with the appropriate time between heating and cooling cycles, the material does not properly reform, and the steel is weakened rather than strengthened.

Similar to how stress or strain can strengthen or weaken steel, stress in the mind can cause one's mental health to be strengthened or weakened. Stresses applied to the mind are similar to steel in that both need the proper conditions to repair the damage that the extreme stress or strain has put on them. They both need the proper conditions to recover from the intense pressure they underwent.

There are two major ways that steel breaks down. One is very slowly over time due to repeated microscopic fractures occurring. The other is rapid because the intense pressure is too great for the material to absorb; it completely breaks in a single incident.

High-cycle fatigue occurs when a material, such as steel, is subjected to low-amplitude, high-frequency elastic strain/stress. If the strain or stress is greater than the material's elastic property/ability to absorb, then microscopic stress fractures occur in the material. Over time, these microfractures continue to expand along the fault line until the material fails under seemingly normal conditions—sometimes hundreds, even thousands, of cycles occur before the part breaks.

Low-cycle fatigue occurs when a part is significantly overstressed, leading to breakage in a single incident of extreme strain or stress. The stress is so great that the part catastrophically fails at the time of the event.

As a safety precaution in aviation, we remove any dynamic component that has exceeded its design stress limits and replace it with a new part to ensure the plane can perform normally. We remove any part that has been subjected to a stress exceeding its design limits and send it to a depot-level maintenance facility. The part is then X-rayed to detect any small microscopic faults in the material. If microscopic cracks are found, the part is retired, or the failed portion is replaced. If no faults or cracks are detected by the X-ray, the part is returned to inventory and service.

I view classic PTSD as similar to low-cycle fatigue in metal. Classic PTSD is a single overwhelming event that greatly dysregulates a person's mental health. Whereas, high-cycle fatigue is similar to Complex PTSD (CPTSD) as it takes significant stress over long periods to develop cracks in the psyche, which develop over an extended period. Chronic unresolved stress is a precursor to CPTSD or a much lesser manifestation of the same mental health dysregulation. These unresolved stresses undermine a person's happiness or mental health, as they did for me.

Therefore, high-stress environments such as combat operations can create microscopic cracks in the mental well-being of our veterans that cause mental and physical health challenges later.

The chronic stress of war or other intense, high-stress occupations or dangerous living conditions can significantly stress the mind and body. While the military goes to great effort to prepare its people for intense emotional situations, no training can fully or adequately prepare everyone for the intense pressure and intense feelings that manifest out of combat experiences. Our history of mental health problems for returning combat veterans tells the untold story and is the true litmus test for the negative effects that high-stress environments, such as war, can inflict upon those who participate.

It is my hope that my analogy will shed light on the complexities of PTSD and how important cognitive processing and times of rest and safety are important to mitigate embodying the stress or trauma.

As I fell deep into my exploration regarding my own trauma, I came across Dr. Gabor Mate giving an interview on a podcast. He discussed how concentration camp survivors and returning war veterans who were children of trauma were much more susceptible to PTSD than people who were brought up in a stable, trauma-free childhood. This, of course, resonated with me. Adult traumatic events have a compounding effect due to the unresolved early childhood trauma (microscopic cracks) in the psyche, which activate or lead to an earlier or more significant mental dysregulation as an adult.

Engaging in daily combat can feel like living in a pressure cooker, where the pressure in the mind builds over time. Without proper pressure relief valves to mitigate the compounding effects. High-stress and high-tempo combat operations or any high-stress or dangerous environment, think first responders, can create a similar, unrecognized impact on the mind, similar to what high-cycle, low-amplitude metal fatigue does for metal.

When one does not recognize the stress, or when it occurs constantly at a low enough level, it can go unnoticed by the individual. When you combine a chronically stressful environment with the bulletproof mentality that comes out of military training, this combination can create the conditions that slowly, subtly dysregulate the minds of the members of the military and other at-risk communities.

Any chronically stressful environment can cause the individual to remain in the sympathetic side of the nervous system for too long. As I mentioned earlier, a nervous system that remains on the sympathetic side can slow down or prevent learning, or healing, thus the slippery slope to emotional autonomic dysregulation or physical health problems begins.

The low-pressure, high-cycle fatigue of any perceived dangerous or intensely stressful environment is the silent fracturer of the mind. In my opinion, the unresolved distress in the minds of combat veterans is a major contributing factor to why many returning veterans commit suicide and why our veteran suicide rate is between 1.5 and 2 times the national rate. They lack understanding of what is going on in their minds or why. I know I didn't understand why I felt the way I did. In fact, on average, over fifteen military veterans take their lives every day. This is a tragedy that can be greatly reduced if we allow for the legal use of psychedelic medicine in conjunction with other health modalities and traditional therapy. The U.S. Veterans Association (VA) has been a vocal and financial supporter of the recent psychedelic clinical trials because it understands the true costs to our nation's military and understands that their current methods of treatment are inadequate.

For some veterans, the daily rocket attacks on their military base were enough for them to chronically not feel safe in their environment. For others, it was going outside the line (base) and conducting missions, like delivering supplies in convoys to the various bases, and fearing an IED attack. For me, it was the fear of going to bed not knowing if I was to be awoken by my father's anger or rage and his belt. While chronic sympathetic 'fight-or-flight' activation can arise from a multitude of sources, the underlying response remains the same: a shift in the person's at-rest nervous system stasis. The longer one is in this environment, the deeper the neural pattern is imprinted in the nervous system, unless mechanisms are employed to counter or mitigate its effects.

Not feeling safe day in and day out keeps the autonomic nervous system on the sympathetic side, which limits our ability to rest, digest, and recover. Over time, it creates a nervous system dysregulation, which sets the conditions for further deterioration of our mental health should major stressors present themselves. It is Complex PTSD, and it is so much harder to identify or to admit having, as was the case with me.

Military service members are not the only at-risk population who are exposed to the chronic stress of not feeling safe in their environment. In the U.S., the Housing and Urban Development (HUD) 2024 Annual Homelessness Assessment Report (AHAR) found that more than 771,000 people lack permanent housing. This creates a similar unsafe feeling in their environment and can trigger many into routine fight-or-flight activation, which becomes their 'dysregulated normal.' Many who find their way to becoming unhoused came from childhood trauma or environments where they did not routinely feel safe, which in turn leads them into a mental health crisis as a young adult or later in life. When this mental emotional dysregulation gets far enough out in the spectrum, it manifests as severe mental illness and or various forms of PTSD, Bipolar or other psychiatric disorders. It is not just a coincidence that many of our unhoused population came from backgrounds of childhood physical or sexual abuse or from broken homes that did not provide the nurturing conditions to thrive.

When it comes to Complex PTSD or chronic stress-related mental health challenges, there is often no singular event that causes a person's mental dysregulation. Instead, the underlying dysregulation stems from a multitude of unresolved disturbances that have built up in their subconscious. These experiences imprint abnormal emotional neural pathways. Small events may cause large reactions because those who suffer from trauma or significant stress already have significant mental stress fractures or subconscious emotional activations. This is why comparing one person's *perspective* with others is the wrong approach.

Strain on the mind happens daily through the stresses of family, work, commuting between home and work, grocery shopping, or even finding a parking space during the Christmas season in a popular shopping center. What separates one person from another is not how much stress ('t' trauma) a person has received, but how well they have been able to process and resolve these stresses, thus releasing their negative effects. If left unresolved, they can build up and eventually lead to emotional dysregulation, as they did for me. How old one is and what cognitive tools the person had at the time will determine their ability to initially resolve. To mitigate or resolve these stress buildups, the individual needs to make time for reflective thought. This requires the person to examine the event with *curiosity* and *compassion*, letting go of the initial distress.

I invite you to examine the stresses in your life and ask yourself how do you deal with stress? Do you hold onto stress longer than necessary? Do you harbor angry energy that does you no benefit? Do you repress your feelings, thus leaving them unresolved? What tools do you use to manage your stress, and do you use them appropriately? Answering these questions, as I did, can go a long way toward understanding who you have become and what you need to work on to be a happier, mentally healthier version of yourself.

Good mental health, at the core, requires feeling safe in your environment. Good mental health requires allowing room to honor your emotions and understand why they manifest. Stress-relieving activities like exercise, breathwork, meditation or prayer, talk therapy (professional or friendship), and many other stress-relieving techniques can be extremely important and effective in maintaining your mental health.

For larger emotional dysregulations or ones that manifest from places you cannot seem to understand or control, I strongly advocate for the use of somatic or EMDR therapy, or even psychedelic medicine under proper guidance and safety protocols. These tools can better resolve some of your deeper trauma triggers or emotional outbursts.

Unfortunately, we cannot take X-rays of the brain and see the same stress cracks or faults in the mind. Nor did we have a legal mental health modality that could quickly find and repair microscopic cracks or dysregulations of the mind . . . until now!

We now have new mental health tools which can help in the reformation of these mental cracks due to intense and constant pressure that is applied to the mind through traumatic or chronic stress. These tools are called psychedelic medicine. These medicines are *psychoplastogens,* meaning they can rapidly promote structural and functional neural plasticity. This neuroplasticity of the brain allows for the reformation of healthy thought patterns, or the elimination of autonomic nervous system activation or triggering. It takes proper integration through deep inner reflection or traditional mental health therapy to repair these cracks. Just Google 'neuroplasticity in the brain psychedelics research' in AI mode, as you will get a detailed rundown on the mechanisms and their potential mental health benefits for those suffering from PTSD, depression, and addiction.

Based on my direct experience, these powerful medicines can open a window on yourself and facilitate rewriting subconscious programming or neural pathways, leading to a happier, mentally healthier version of yourself. Under the right conditions, they can be a valuable tool for detecting and resolving aspects of your human experience that have programmed negative patterns or beliefs . . . even ones you have hidden from yourself, like me.

Recent clinical studies have shown that psychedelic medicines allow the brain the neuroplasticity to heal the mental stress cracks which trigger emotional dysregulation at a higher success rate, and in much less time than traditional talk therapy alone. Psychedelic medicine is similar to reheating the metal during the forging process to reform in a stronger, more resilient way.

Key elements to psychedelic medicine effectiveness are:

- The Right SET (mindset) and SETTING (safe and stable environment)
- Thoughtful INTENTION (ask the right question)
- Allow yourself compassion to INTEGRATE properly. (Love or accept whatever comes up)

These medicines, under the right conditions, can rewire our subconscious, emotional default mode network, and autonomic emotional responses toward a better, more relaxed state. A good analogy that I resonate with is that a therapeutic journey under psychedelic medicine is like ten years of therapy utilizing traditional methods. You can achieve so much more in a much shorter timeline if you are properly guided and allow for proper integration.

However, these powerful medicines, when used in the wrong set or setting, can wreak havoc on the brain, doing as much damage as they can do good. These medicines do not distinguish good or bad. It is the environment that makes this distinction. With great power comes great responsibility, and thus these powerful medicines need to be treated with reverence and care.

If we, as a species, will universally allow psychedelic medicines to be legally administered, under the right conditions and with the appropriate safety protocols, we can unblock, unwind, and 're-normalize' our fellow humans to a much greater extent and with quicker results.

This I Know!

11

WAR AND COMBAT

Combat is a Rite of Passage: Anyone who participates in combat cannot return to who they were before. A Rite of Passage can embolden and empower, or it can isolate and imprison. The key is radical acceptance, fully accepting without judgment that combat is where injustices are met with further injustices as a means of protection or survival.

While I am not going to go into any detail about the ugliness of war, I will address it on a macro level. Combat is where injustices are met with more injustices as a means of survival or protection in a violent and extremely destructive way on all sides. There is no right or wrong side-both sides are destroying the lives of loved ones, which negatively ripples into their respective communities. These negative effects create the conditions for the next injustice, and the next injustice, as humanity keeps rehashing unresolved traumas that get embodied from the previous injustice. Humanity is caught in a trauma cycle.

Those who engage in combat and survive generally do not come out of the engagement better human beings because combat is an ugly and destructive endeavor, and this destructive or chaotic energy gets stored in all those who participate if we do not fully process and release it. In today's modern combat, the scars of war may not be as readily visible on the physical body as was the case in ancient history, but killing others or witnessing the death of those around you does carry a burden that weighs heavily on the minds and hearts of those who participate or witness. These memories, along with the associated emotions of anger or rage, fear, sadness, or helplessness, as well as others, get stored in the bodies of those involved.

As you can imagine, daily combat is a highly tense and emotional situation that triggers a rapid surge of adrenaline and other regulatory hormones. This large dose of adrenaline, in response to an emerging or immediate threat, imparts extreme stress on the body and nervous system. This shot of adrenaline can be euphoric and routine, as it was for me. When the airhorn tone that signaled my mission of the day was being called into action, I would get an immediate rush of energy. After many days of being called to respond quickly, I was conditioned like Pavlov's dog, salivating at the sound of the dinner bell. Combat became automatic . . . became natural . . . became 'normal' for us.

The stresses of combat can raise dopamine levels as well as other emotional neurotransmitters to levels that are ten to one hundred times what is considered normal. This somewhat daily rush of stress-related neurotransmitters would make me feel really, truly alive. One feels really powerful when in this emotional state.

Another effect from the rush of adrenaline that accompanies combat or any traumatic experience is that the emotions that accompany the event can get threaded into and locked into your memories because they are more than you can process, thus, let go of . . . at the time.

The rush of anger that floods your nervous system when someone is shooting at you provides you with the energy to fight back. The rush of rage and disgust of seeing someone being killed in horrific ways gets embedded in the memory. These trapped emotions become the emotional pain that one carries into their future. They set up a neural pathway that can be activated by seemingly unrelated events. It is these stored emotions and the programming or imprinting they impart that the person does not seem to be in control of, nor understand. Then the pattern of confusion, anger, or beratement, or even worse, self-hatred, accompanies these memories, which then cause the person to engage in self-harm through addictions, violent outbursts due to anger or rage . . . OR! I could go on and on, but each combat or capital "T" traumatic experience holds its own unique feelings or frequencies, captured like an insect frozen in time and preserved in amber. Anytime an experience becomes emotionally overwhelming, we either absorb, thus embody, or we purge, scream, or shake it out. We, by design, all hold on to some of the overflow of emotions that accompany traumatic events because we are wired to retain these events as a means of learning or future protection.

As I look back to my childhood and the experience of watching my father drive home, after experiencing his own father trying to kill him . . . for the second time, I now realize that I witnessed my father embody and lock in the anger and rage he felt. I can still see him raging due to the pain he felt while internally berating himself for being so stupid as to allow it to happen again. I can see this in him because I used to do the same to myself when I made any serious mistake.

This human mechanism helps us learn not to repeat serious mistakes. Unfortunately, we were not designed to have these experiences over and over again, but this is what combat or other chronically dangerous or extremely stressful environments provide us.

When looking at the effects of extreme stress, and the deep ingraining of neural responses, we see that they establish pathways in the brain which prime our combat veterans to be hypervigilant or hyper aware and hyper in-tune with their *surroundings*. Sound familiar? The more combat a person experiences, the deeper and wider these neural highways become, and the more dysregulated they can become. This is because the nervous system has been altered enough times that the combat veterans and other at-risk communities' emotional baseline shifts strongly toward the sympathetic or 'fight-or-flight' side and ingrains triggering criteria to activate. It does this to respond quickly to an emerging threat. The best measure I know of to assess or understand a person's autonomic nervous system stasis at rest is Heart Rate Variability (HRV), which I discussed earlier.

In addition to having an unbalanced nervous system. Another stress response the body may do to adjust to chronic stress is to lower the 'at stasis' level of certain neurotransmitters like dopamine. The brain recognizes that it cannot hit the dopamine button over and over again and get the results it needs, so the body tunes down or lowers the 'at-rest' levels of dopamine and other neurochemicals.

As I mentioned earlier, it appeared that my brother had low dopamine levels due to the chronically elevated stress of our childhood home. Low dopamine levels put the person at higher risk for depression, drug addiction, and mood swings. My brother has struggled with all these his entire life, as I believe that this is a mechanism that fed into his mental instability and drug addiction. A similar dysregulation occurs in some of our returning combat veterans.

The longer one is in an elevated stressful environment, the more the body tries to adapt. Over time, this stressful environment can instill a new normal and ingrain new thought patterns, emotional regulatory states, or neurotransmitter levels that do not necessarily fit with what is required in a 'normal', less dangerous society. According to the National Library of Medicine, the average lifespan for U.S. veterans with 100% service-connected disability is approximately 67 years, which is over a decade younger than the general population.

In a combat veteran's adjusted normal, any mistake can be life-or-death; thus, the heightened nervous system or shifted default mode network is a coping mechanism that helps ensure their safety in a combat environment. Unfortunately, these neurochemical changes can cause returning veterans to overreact to situations with their families, friends, or coworkers. Veterans who carry this sense of urgency back home to their families struggle to reacclimate to a life where mistakes are not life-threatening. How do I know this? I carried this energy back to my family.

From what I have recently learned by first-hand experience, psychedelic medicine can be an important part of this emotional and neurological resetting. Psychedelic medicine should be considered as a legal tool to help release this conditioning and to reset our combat veterans' emotional state back to a calmer, more relaxed homeostasis.

We have only just begun to understand and crack this code. Still, I am a true believer that psychedelic medicines can play a very important role in this emotional default network reset—for not only our returning veterans but also other at-risk communities like first responders, the chronically unhoused, domestic violence or child abuse sufferers, and many others.

The tools that have been the most successful in addressing these issues for me are the ones I never thought I would consider, due to drugs being the cause of my family's dysfunction. From my early point of view, drugs were the cause of a significant amount of my family's troubles. Yet, psychedelic drugs are the ones that have helped me the most.

A non-profit organization called VETS (Veterans Exploring Treatment Solutions) is sending our nation's special forces to global locations (due to current U.S. laws) to utilize various forms of psychedelic medicine in a therapeutic setting to reset the emotional autonomic nervous system and emotional default mode network back to what it was before partaking in and witnessing the horrors of combat. They are successfully returning our Special Forces to a happier, healthier state of consciousness.

I find it shameful that our country is not willing to legally provide our nation's war heroes the medicine they deserve. As Richard Schwartz's book *No Bad Parts* describes, sometimes parts of us have to act in very destructive ways to protect the whole. This is what our military combat veterans do. We do the nasty work so that others may live a safer, more peaceful life. This does not make us bad people; we are put in difficult roles which require life or death decisions.

Let us provide a legal mechanism to allow these good people who served honorably in very difficult and deadly situations to be able to return to the loving, caring, happy people they were prior to engaging in the destructive acts that war requires.

This I Know!

12

CHRONIC STRESS OF COMBAT OPERATIONS

The mind, without mechanisms to reduce or resolve the disturbances of life, creates the conditions for unseen mental cracks to form in the psyche, which can manifest as physical and mental health issues.

The Marine Corps adopted a seven-month combat tour for those engaged in direct-action combat, like I was. The Army chose to rotate its members for 12-month deployments, regardless of whether they served in a direct action or a supporting or staff role. At first, the Marine Corps set the time at home between combat tours at 5.5 months. This short turnaround time was due to a manpower shortage that took a couple of years to resolve. Once the manpower shortage was resolved, the Marine Corps moved to a seven-month deployment and eleven months at-home cycle for those involved in direct-action combat. For Marines not engaged in direct action, a 12-month deployment and 12-month at-home schedule was adhered to, similar to the Army's.

It would be an interesting study to examine how the Army's approach affected the mental health of its returning combat veterans versus the Marine Corps approach. I am biased, but believe that a shorter combat period is better as long as the time between deployments is adequate, ideally at least double the time deployed to a combat zone, because the operational tempo was, at times . . . intense.

The body naturally adjusts baseline neurochemical homeostasis in response to the elevated stress of living in a wartime environment. Thus, the need to reset the individual back into a lower stress, safe environment to mitigate any long-term mental health effects that sustained combat can impart.

Before I went to Iraq for the first time, a beloved Captain who worked for me knocked on my office door after a flight. He asked if he could shut the door and speak with me privately. After he shut the door, he broke down in tears. He told me that the only reason he did not fly the aircraft into the ground or into his wingman and commit suicide was that he cared for the other pilots in both aircraft more than he wished to die.

He had completed three combat tours, and he was preparing to go on his fourth combat tour in about as many years (seven months combat, followed by 5.5 months home; seven months of combat followed by 5.5 months home; seven months of combat followed by eleven months home, and was scheduled to go back for seven more months of combat). He informed me how he had been drinking to mask his pain, and how his wife was getting ready to leave him due to his alcohol consumption and not being emotionally available in their relationship and to his family.

I was taken aback by his confession, but I could visibly see the mental anguish he was in. I let him know that, although I had not experienced what he had, it was OK and that he was OK. I let him know that he was not weak but that he just did not have the cognitive tools to address and process the horrors of war. I tried to soothe him and assure him that it wasn't his fault, but the fault of a system that was overburdened. I told him we were going to get him help getting the tools he needed to put himself back together. I gave him a strong and caring hug as he wept on my shoulder. Afterward, I arranged for him to go to a level three alcohol rehabilitation program, and he was removed from service. He never flew for the Marine Corps again.

This story is not unique, nor unexpected. The human mind can only handle so much continual stress or strain before it needs time to repair. This cognitive repair requires the proper conditions; otherwise, the stress fractures of the mind build, as they did for this quality Marine. Similar to how steel is weakened during the forging process, if the cooling and repair cycle is not properly controlled or long enough.

The demands of war and our high operational tempo broke this high-quality Marine to the point he was no longer fit for service. This was not his fault, but the fault of a system that was trying to quickly adapt to a large-scale, long-term military operation on the opposite side of the globe with limited trained personnel. Everyone knew the initial Marine Corps deployment schedule was not sustainable. This is why significant effort was put into doubling the at-home period between deployments for us 'trigger pullers.' Unfortunately, returning people from staff positions to flying status took time, and some of our Marines paid the price by taking on more than their fair share of the combat burden.

For this, I will always be grateful to this Marine and others like him.

I was one of those who left a staff position early to get back into the cockpit and help alleviate this manpower shortfall. Our operational tempo was extremely fast, but was much more manageable due to the eleven-month rotation at-home.

To shed light on what a seven-month deployment to Iraq looked like as a Cobra attack helicopter pilot, my combat experience was 12 hours on, 12 hours off, 7 days a week, for 7 months straight, without a single day off. In actuality, twelve-hour workdays were fourteen-hour workdays due to the requirement to prep, brief, and gear up before taking the twelve-hour shift in the aircraft. After the twelve-hour shift was over, we had to record the missions flown and debrief our intelligence folks, as well as the oncoming crews, on what had happened, what was seen, and what was learned. Additionally, due to the extreme heat in the summer and the extreme stress we were under, our flight suits would routinely be completely soaked with sweat after our missions. Days were both physically and mentally exhausting.

Our flight missions lasted anywhere from 30 minutes to 2 hours, and we could be flying for up to six and one-half hours a day, conducting mission after mission after mission. On occasion, we would rotate another crew to take over on the battlefield while the original crew came back to base to refuel or reload weapons. We had one butt per seat, meaning we had no extra people to backfill should someone get hurt or sick. In these circumstances, we had to borrow from in-country staff commands to fill this void because we had a schedule to keep.

My first tour was from April to October 2006. Some of our missions were preplanned and thus scheduled, while others were immediate due to combat breaking out in our Area of Responsibility (AOR).

For immediate-need missions such as Casualty Evacuation (CASEVAC) or Troops in Contact (TIC)/a.k.a. firefight, we had two different airhorn tones that the operations officer could activate and that could be heard throughout our squadron and flightline. The airhorn would alert the maintenance personnel and designated aircrews of the emerging mission. The aircrews assigned to the mission would immediately respond to the airhorn by sprinting out to their assigned aircraft. We would run to the aircraft, don our flight gear, Kevlar vests with hard Kevlar armor, and jump into the aircraft. The pilot in the rear seat would start the aircraft and turn on all flight-related and aircraft-survivability systems, whereas the pilot in the front seat would turn on the radios, receive mission tasking from the operations officer, and activate the aircraft's weapons systems. We were very efficient in this and would be airborne within a few minutes of the initial airhorn.

We flew a set six-day repeating schedule, designed to provide pilots with easier missions on days that followed the most difficult or mentally taxing missions. We called our schedule the 'flight ladder.'

Day 1: Casualty Evacuation or CASEVAC 1: The mission was to escort a utility aircraft (Huey or Blackhawk) and provide overhead weapons coverage so the injured military member could be picked up by the utility aircraft and airlifted to a Combat Surgical Hospital (CSH) located in Baghdad or Balad in an effort to save their life.

Day 2: General Support: This day was for preplanned missions with a set schedule. You would provide overhead visual support and weapons to troops on the ground. A significant portion of the time, it was ground convoy escort or route clearance. We would look for Improvised Explosive Devices (IEDs) along their route or hiding places for the enemy to ambush the convoy. At other times, General Support involved supporting Military Operations in Urban Terrain (MOUT) when the personnel on the ground would go through certain sections of a city (Ramadi, Fallujah, Karma . . .) On occasion, we would be tasked to provide overhead weapons support to Other Defense Agencies (ODA) (think Seals, Delta Force, or other unnamed agencies) to extract or eliminate high-value enemy individuals during late-night or early-morning raids. We would act as the overhead eyes and guns to support their missions.

Day 3: Casualty Evacuation 2: Same as CASEVAC 1, but you were the second crew going out during your shift this day.

Day 4: Strip Alert: When military members on the ground were being shot at on missions that did not have dedicated air support, the section of aircraft assigned to this mission would respond to a distinctive airhorn that was different than the one used for CASEVAC missions. This immediate tasking could be received, and our aircraft would be airborne within 3 to 4 minutes. Fallujah was only a 5–6-minute flight, whereas Ramadi was about 12 minutes, so we could quickly get into the fight.

Day 5: CASEVAC 3: More casualty evacuation, but the third crew to go out during this shift. On occasion, we could have all three CASEVAC crews out at the same time.

Day 6: (Flex day): This was the only day that you were not flying combat-related missions. Depending on the position and ground job responsibilities, this day was reserved to accomplish the officer's ground job. I was a maintenance pilot, so on these days I performed post-maintenance testing to ensure the aircraft would perform as expected. If the aircraft passed the testing regime, it could be returned to the inventory of aircraft available for combat tasking. If you were lucky enough, you could get in a workout on this day off and go to the chow hall and get a hot meal.

Our Squadron repeated this six-day pattern each day for the entire deployment. It was meant to provide stability and continuity to our days and weeks. There were some days when we would have all of our aircraft and aircrews all flying at the same time because the 'business of combat was so good.' Our pilots would encounter missions that were quite memorable and may have required time to cognitively process, but the tempo of flight operations did not allow for it. What does a good Marine aviator do? We compartmentalize—another term for shoving combat-related stress down and out of consciousness—so we can stay focused on the task at hand to protect and serve. Military pilots are some of the best at compartmentalization because we teach this skill from the start as a survival mechanism.

As I described earlier: aviate, navigate, communicate. In that order . . . Specifically! Keep the Aircraft flying (Primary). Navigate to a safe space or, if able, toward your goal, and if and only if you still have any left-over mental capacity . . . you communicate to others your intent or what you need them to do. There is no fourth step: process the event, because cognitive processing is not required for survival. So, what happens to the stress of combat missions? Typically, it gets shoved down and out of our consciousness because today we are only trying to survive and serve. And tomorrow . . . more of the same. We were in and out of potentially dangerous situations throughout the combat deployment, as this reality became our new 'normal'.

What I didn't realize until recently was that all the unresolved stress was stored in my subconscious and in my body. When you couple these high-tempo combat operations with:

- Somewhat daily rocket attacks by the enemy on your base that are random in timing and location.
- The stress of being away from family, missing birthdays, Christmases . . . and the 'normal' stresses that life delivers.

Repressed emotions and unresolved disturbances of our veterans' minds tend to build up over time. In fact, I missed my daughter's birth and subsequent four birthdays due to operational tempo, even though no wars were taking place during this time.

According to Dr. Barbara Fredrickson, a positivity researcher at the University of North Carolina, for every heart-wrenching negative emotional experience you endure, you need to experience at least three heartfelt positive emotional experiences that uplift you to counterbalance their effects. This is because we are hard-wired to remember our strongly negative emotional events as a survival mechanism. Combat operations, as you can imagine, can create a large emotional deficit to this happiness quotient.

Additionally, the base we were on would get attacked with rockets on an almost-daily basis during my first tour to Iraq. Granted, Al Taqaddum Air Base was very large, and the rockets were neither strategic nor accurate, so the actual risk was very minimal, according to a mathematical equation.

We Marines have a sick sense of humor, which helps us process the insanity of war. I remember joking with other pilots as we would watch everyone scramble for safety when the air raid sirens went off to alert us that our base was being attacked with rockets. Our porta-potties were only a short walk away, but initially had no Hesco-barrier protection. We would promise each other that if we were sitting on the porta-potty and were killed by an incoming rocket during our 'sit-down performance,' the official report would not include mention of this action during our death.

The somewhat daily questioning of our odds of randomly getting the 'lottery win' was joked about. While morbid, we had to have conversations and tell jokes about different scenarios that could cause our deaths. In other words, this humor kept us human as we dealt with death on an almost-daily basis, which, as you can imagine, can carry significant weight on our people's minds.

Most people, when faced with danger, instinctively run away. We, Marine aviators, were taught and conditioned to run into danger. Every time the air horns would go off, when it was our turn, we would sprint to our aircraft like dogs salivating at the empty ring of Pavlov's training bell. In our version of this conditioning response, we would run and fly headfirst into the most dangerous situations, willingly and with the utmost determination, to support those in a much worse situation than our own.

In fact, I was so indoctrinated by this conditioned response that after I returned from my first tour to Iraq, I was home for only a few days, and I heard an emergency siren while walking out of the grocery store with my family. Immediately upon hearing the siren, my body flooded me with a huge shot of adrenaline and other neurotransmitters, preparing me to jump into action. As my body was flooded with these chemicals, they triggered my brain to be hypervigilant. So, before my mind could register what the sound was, my mind and body were already prepping me for action. My subconscious automatically gave me the adrenaline it thought I would need. To be perfectly honest, it was a little disorienting as I did not know why I had responded this way at the time.

Still to this day, but to a much lesser extent, I can still get a similar automatic flood of endorphins and body response when a siren or loud bang happens close to me. It is woven into my subconscious and has become a part of me. If you have similar reactions to sights, sounds, or smells, Eye Movement Desensitization and Reprocessing (EMDR) is a therapeutic tool that can reduce or eliminate these subconscious activations.

Now that I understand this conditioning response, I chuckle and tell myself, *Thank you for alerting me -nice work, but everything is okay . . . Now.*

This helps me honor my past while responding to the present. It is when embarrassment, shame, or other negative emotional responses meet this conditioning response that reinforce its negative effect.

This I Know!

13

COMPOUNDING UNRESOLVED STRESSES AND THEIR EFFECTS

Chronic unresolved mental stressors deteriorate mental and physical health by adding to the daily stressors of one's life. Their combined effects can lead to chronic health conditions, which may seem unrelated but are contributory.

When it comes to chronic stress, there is not one event that one can trace to the mental malfunction, dysregulation, or outburst, chronic fatigue, constant anxiety . . . or whatever your stress response flavor is. These small but recurring stressors create the underlying conditions that trigger changes in hormonal and neurochemical levels, which manifest as emotional dysregulation of the autonomic nervous system. In other words, chronic stress lessens our ability to handle additional stress.

What may seem like a small event to some may create significant disturbances/disruptions to others. Because they already have significant stress fractures of the mind, or unprocessed past events in their lives, leading up to a perceived 'over-reaction' to a stimulus.

I had a roommate in college who, anytime a severe storm would come, would go into 'prepper mode.' He would run to the grocery store, put non-perishable items in bins, and spread them throughout the house and his vehicle. He would bottle water, put pillows and blankets in the bathtub, and use a large piece of plywood to cover it. Is this rational behavior for a normal person? No, it is not. The reason he did this was that his house was struck and torn apart by a tornado when he was a small child. Now, does this behavior seem 'normal'?

On the opposite end, what may seem like a major event can end up seeming normal or can become normal. For me, responding to the almost-daily airhorns was, in some ways, exhilarating. The rush of neurotransmitters, such as adrenaline and dopamine, rushing through my body felt amazing at the time. It made me feel powerful!! A study found that combat can raise dopamine levels up to 100 times normal levels. Chronically elevated dopamine levels that happen when you are in daily combat or in any extremely high-stress environment for a considerable period are not sustainable. Therefore, your body depresses the 'at-rest' levels in order to tune down the system so that you can better sustain. The mind and body can't keep hitting the dopamine button over and over and over again, so the amygdala down-regulates your homeostatic 'at-rest' level of these hormones in order to maintain their positive effect.

When a person has been in a long-term, chronically stressful environment that activated the amygdala to downregulate their stress response system, and is then removed from that environment. The person's at-rest dopamine level is now below normal. The body has neurochemically adjusted to the chronically stressful environment. Chronic low dopamine function has been associated with increased risk for PTSD. So, the body's natural regulatory mechanism prepares for future emotional imbalance should a traumatic situation arise later.

Low dopamine levels also lead to several factors of depression, including lack of motivation or drive, lack of concentration, moodiness, and anxiety. Low dopamine also makes the individual much more susceptible to drug and alcohol abuse, as I believe this natural body regulatory mechanism did for my brother. This is also the trap many of our returning veterans fall into, as it may have been the case for the Captain who came into my office crying.

For military members who were stationed in an extremely stressful combat environment, this environment can lead to the need for chronic stress to feel normal. This is why many military members volunteer to go back to the combat environment time and time again. In a sense, they are getting addicted to chronic stress as this becomes the new normal due to adjusting to this higher stress environment. In fact, I knew a few Marines who fell into this category, which prompted the Marine Corps to implement policies to address the issue. This downregulating mechanism may also explain why many returning veterans engage in high-risk activities.

As I was completing my flight refresher training and before I went to Iraq the first time, I was tasked as the Director of Safety and Standardization for all the squadrons stationed at Camp Pendleton, CA. As we were analyzing the safety statistics of our returning combat veterans, a statistic that jumped out to me was the motorcycle accident rate.

For returning veterans, this rate was twice the historical rate these squadrons had shown. The chronic stress that these combat veterans were under may have caused a downregulation of the stress response nervous system. Once the veterans returned to society, and with a lowered homeostatic level of the stress hormones, this downregulated emotional response caused them to engage in higher-risk events like high-speed motorcycle racing.

For returning veterans whose stress response system has been downregulated, and they are now back in a less stressful environment, it takes a higher level of stress in order to produce the normal amount of dopamine. This is how risk junkies are born. I am sure we would have been able to directly tie our increased motorcycle accident rate to a downregulated stress response system in several of our motorcycle accident victims if we had the ability to test and monitor. Many of the new smart watches can test HRV, Sleep Scores, Training Readiness, etc. These tools could help us understand how high-stress environments affect our people.

Many returning veterans who do not engage in activities that help them to overcome this downregulation fall into a state of depression. In the late 2000s, I noticed a significant increase in overweight military members after they returned from war. Could the extreme stress these people were under contribute to this phenomenon? While I do not have direct evidence of the cause, I believe the two factors are at least correlated, if not causal.

This depressive effect is exacerbated when leaving service, since civilian life can typically be a much less stressful environment than our military members experienced while on Active Duty. No longer do many have the same stressors that kept their dopamine levels within or closer to normal ranges. Low stress leads to low dopamine production and low motivation, which can lead to high anxiety or depression. Looking back as I write this, I think I exhibited and expressed this chemical imbalance, which contributed to my PTSD flaring up after leaving service, as I felt extremely depressed upon returning to my hometown.

I tell the story of combat veterans because this is the population I know, but the physiological effects of chronic stress are not just a veteran-of-war issue. In fact, chronic stress permeates our society at all levels. Many of our homeless or unhoused population or domestic violence population are living in a chronic state of stress. Sports figures who operate at the top of their game, like Simone Biles, can find themselves in a chronic stress environment, which can become overwhelming. This is a problem that needs to be part of the conversation around the mental health crisis that we are currently in, and desperately needs to be addressed as a nation and as a species.

If you look at humans from an evolutionary perspective, we are not genetically designed for chronic stress. In fact, we are hard-wired to hold on to stress because, in the natural world, severe stress is rare, and when it does occur, it is very important to our survival to hold on to and learn from it.

For many people, our bio-psycho-social environment is toxic due to the excess stress of daily life. The stress of not being able to earn enough money to feed your family, the stress of losing your job, the stress of . . . name your top three to five stressors!!! When stress is held onto and not let go of, it lessens one's ability to take on more. Eventually, everyone will reach a point at which they are unable to cope with the normal stresses of everyday life . . . as I did. I repressed my emotions and stress and shoved them down and kept piling on more until it interfered with my ability to function on a daily basis. I had a hoarder's basement of lost memories and repressed emotions, which sat unresolved in my consciousness. I had done just like my parents had done and effectively taught me.

On a daily basis, we utilize techniques, knowingly or unknowingly, to reduce or suppress our stressors. There are negative methods one uses to cope with daily life stress, like alcohol, cutting, or binge eating, to name a few. They work in the short term to soothe the mind and ease the pain, but in the long term, they only reinforce the root causes that led to the behavior in the first place. One must identify the root cause of the stress or pain to stop these negative behaviors. Getting to the root cause can be very difficult because we are really good at lying to ourselves (protector parts) or the memories are hidden from our consciousness, as they were for me.

More research needs to be done on veterans returning from war, chronically unhoused or incarcerated populations, and how these extremely stressful environments affect the emotional regulatory nervous system long-term. While we know that chronic stress is linked to macroscopic changes in certain brain areas, consisting of volume variations and physical modifications of neuronal networks. These changes are known to have a connection to depression and PTSD, although a definitive cause-and-effect relationship is not fully understood from the research I was able to conduct.

I would love to see a study of the autonomic nervous system, default mode network, and the hormonal neurotransmitters, such as dopamine levels, of our special forces and military members before combat and how their levels adjust after combat, both in the short and long term. I think a similar study of the chronically unhoused or high-security incarcerated population would yield similar results.

With this knowledge, we should utilize the legal tools we have to better identify those at risk. Additionally, I would like to help direct a clinical study that puts these same at-risk individuals through an intensive psychedelic trauma release and reintegration program similar to a thirty-day rehab program. The goal would be to restore their baseline neurochemical state to a more relaxed, balanced state. This way, we can return our fellow citizens' nervous systems to a calmer state so they can better integrate back into society.

As I reflect upon my healing journey, I believe that too much attention is placed on the symptoms or manifestations of our problems. They fail to address what is really at the root of various subconscious behaviors. For many of us, it is unresolved or unprocessed emotions and pain from our past! Alcoholics initially drink, not because they are addicted to alcohol (although there is a physical aspect of alcohol dependency that develops over time). They drink because alcohol masks the feelings of inadequacy, anxiety, fear, shame, or other negative emotions. This socially accepted coping mechanism is initially useful as it provides short-term relief. Initially, alcohol soothes these negative emotions as it becomes the easy button for the stresses of daily life. The problem arises when it is used too often or as a tool to avoid or mask your emotions, rather than processing them and letting them go. In this case, alcohol creeps into their lives and adds to the problems they are using alcohol to mask. Over time, this initial successful coping mechanism can progress from social drinker to functional alcoholic to non-functional alcoholic, as it did for my mother.

When it becomes chronic, the negative effects begin to add up. What was once a subtractor of pain now becomes a multiplier of pain, because too much pain or repressed feelings stack up, which overwhelms the positive effects alcohol, or other drug of choice, initially provided. If you are a heavy consumer of alcohol, a cannabis or tobacco smoker, I challenge you to shift your focus from one of checking 'out' to one of checking 'in'. Ask yourself, *Why am I reaching for said [drug of choice]?* How do I feel in this moment? What do I need to bring into my life, or what do I need to resolve or let go of? Is there another healthier or more productive coping mechanism I can employ?

If you find yourself severely addicted or addicted to strong drugs like heroin or methamphetamine, then ayahuasca and ibogaine are two extremely powerful plant medicines that have been shown to have profound effects to address and remove the root causes of severe addiction problems. The founder of Rythmia in Costa Rica had a serious drug addiction problem, which he resolved through psychedelic plant medicine (Ibogaine), and led him to open the medical facility, which uses ayahuasca as its medicine. Ron White, the comedian, talks openly about his struggle with alcohol and how his ayahuasca experience has profoundly changed his relationship with alcohol. Additionally, the founder of Alcoholics Anonymous (AA) took part in an LSD study, which led him to create the 12-step program, which is the foundation of AA.

See the pattern?

The name of the game is to process, thus let go of the negative thoughts and feelings that accompany what your negative human experiences have given you. A young person without much life experience cannot be expected to have the cognitive tools to address what an adult generally can be expected to have. Similarly, an adult like my father, who had severe early childhood unresolved trauma, cannot be expected to use the cognitive tools his adult brain might understand when those unresolved childhood memories are activated, a.k.a., his rage is triggered to blackout.

He is, effectively, a small child in a man's body until his fight-or-flight response has subsided and his nervous system rebalances. My father never properly developed the cognitive tools or provided himself the space to heal from his trauma because he did not believe in, nor give himself the gift of, mental health therapy. This is why he never moved past these early, painful, and disturbing childhood events and why he unwittingly passed them on to his children, whom he loved the best he could. Unfortunately, it wasn't very well. In other words, my father could not be the amazing, loving human he was at his core when he was holding onto so many unresolved traumas and pains, which activated his bad behavior.

For many of us, we are unable to go into these painful memories without being put back into a place of fear or panic. When in this emotional state, parts of the brain are shut down, which, unfortunately, are the parts you need to be active in order to resolve the original traumatic event. As I stated at the beginning of this memoir, safety is at the root of healing. The set and setting for this inner work are extremely important to the person's success. As I reflect on my own healing and learn more about the recent Phase-three clinical trials utilizing psilocybin and MDMA, I can say with complete honesty that these aspects are imperative to one's success.

Comparing one person's behavior with another's is the wrong approach. Stress and strain on the mind occur daily through the pressures of family, work, commuting between home and work, grocery shopping, and finding a parking space.

What separates one person from another is not how much stress a person has received. What separates one person from another is the cognitive tools they had at the time and how well they have processed their experiences since.

This I Know!

14

CASEVAC MISSIONS WERE THE WORST

Witnessing trauma, also known as vicarious trauma or secondary trauma, involves being exposed to a traumatic event without directly experiencing it. Both can lead to PTSD, but research suggests unique brain changes may occur in those who witness trauma compared to those who experience it directly, potentially requiring different treatment approaches.

Casualty evacuation (CASEVAC) missions were some of the most difficult missions for me because these missions forced us to emotionally sit in the horrors of war. Being an overhead escort while picking up a wounded military member and trying to rush them to safety were emotionally powerful missions for me. They were also some of the most diverse missions.

On one occasion, we were called to escort an 'angel' as part of our CASEVAC responsibilities. An 'angel' flight is where we transfer a dead body to Combat Surgical Hospital (CSH) Balad or CSH Bagdad to be further transported out of the country and back to the U.S. and their families.

On this particular day, the Blackhawk crew and I landed at Forward Operating Base (FOB) Ramadi. As we are sitting on the ground awaiting the dead body, we see a person deliver a fourteen-inch by fourteen-inch box to the aircraft. We assume it is just some of the daily mail or items exchanged between bases as additional cargo. The Blackhawk crew we are escorting calls for takeoff. I can't remember who asked whom . . . but one of us asked the other, "Did you see the body?" as neither of us saw a body bag delivered to the aircraft. We confirmed with the Blackhawk crew that what was left of the body was in the small box.

In this moment, my heart sank as my mind immediately rushed back to the mission I responded to the previous day, where a convoy was attacked with an IED. As I came upon the scene, I witnessed a large hole in the road with a debris field of mangled metal strewn about for thirty or more feet from the large and deep crater. It took me a few seconds to mentally understand that what I was looking at was a destroyed Humvee. It was blown apart so much that it was unrecognizable. Immediately, I recognized that the person in that small box had been in the Humvee the day before, and my heart broke a little that day.

This flight had no communications except when the Blackhawk crew called for landing at the destination. During these flights, you sit in silence, contemplating how precious life is. Your heart goes out to their families and what they must be going through. You think about your own family and how grateful you are to still be alive. No words can adequately describe the somber tone of these flights and the deep remorse felt by all who participate in ensuring they get back to their families and to a much more peaceful resting place. Like I said . . . CASEVAC missions gave me the worst disruptions to my consciousness because I was forced to sit in the horrors of combat.

The only missions worse than 'angel' missions were CASEVAC missions, which turned into 'angel' flights. On a rare occasion, we would get a CASEVAC mission which, after pickup, required the Blackhawk helicopter crew to fly as fast as they could because the wounded patient's vital signs were collapsing. The Blackhawk crew would let us know that the patient was red-lining and would pull max power.

A Blackhawk (UH-60) at max power is slightly faster than the AH-1W. During this flight profile, we would see them very slowly pull away from us as we flew toward the Combat Surgical Hospital. We did not mind being left behind, as seconds count in this situation. We were there to make sure that if the Blackhawk was attacked, we would clean up and deter the enemy from attacking one of our aircraft again. Whenever we saw the Blackhawk drop its tail and slow down to allow us to catch up and be in a tighter formation, we instinctively knew that the patient had died. Each time, my mind rushed back to thoughts of my children, my wife, my extended family, and friends. Each and every time, a piece of my heart broke and rebroke for those who had just passed, and I was truly grateful for just being alive. Gratitude . . . Gratitude . . . Gratitude.

Lyrics from the Song Gratitude by Londrelle:

I've got to be thankful because someone lost their life today
And so every moment I endeavor to live life the righteous way.
To serve with a sense of purpose and let love light the way
. . .
I appreciate my life, Ase
I appreciate my breath, Ase
I appreciate my sight, Ase

The loss of their life was not lost on us, and their deaths weighed heavily on our hearts. At the same time, I also felt a sense of honor that I was there when they died and was there to appreciate their life, even if I did not know them. I felt honored to be a small part of the process that ensured they would be returned to their loved ones. Even though I never met them, I didn't know their names, beliefs, or even their political affiliations (if any). What I knew was that they were humans doing the best they could, with what they knew at the time, so their death demanded my everlasting respect.

On another occasion, while I was briefly stationed in Al Qaim, Iraq, I was tasked with responding to a Troops in Contact mission, which turned into a CASEVAC pickup. One of the casualties brought back to our base was a wounded enemy combatant who was in the firefight I was called out to support.

A couple of hours after I returned to the base, I was walking by the medical section on my way to make a phone call. In this hallway, I witnessed a senior Marine officer scream at and berate a doctor who had just spent hours in surgery to save the life of that enemy combatant. The senior officer was irate at the doctor because the individual (enemy) whom the doctor had saved had potentially killed a couple of his men. Two of our men were lost that day.

The doctor rightfully fired back, "You should have finished the job if you didn't want me to save him." It was the doctor's right and duty to save all human lives presented to him. In fact, it is part of his Hippocratic Oath. Both people were irate, and they had to be separated.

As I witnessed the senior Marine unleash his emotional pain on the doctor, I understood the grief that the commanding officer was in. It was painfully obvious that his heart and soul had been ripped apart by the events of the day. Seeing his pain and anger was profoundly meaningful to me.

When someone's heart is deeply wounded, it can be overwhelming. Some lock the pain deep into their body and subconscious, as I witnessed my father do. While others purge the feeling back out because it can be too overwhelming for the person to fully hold onto. Unfortunately, this senior officer took out his pain on the doctor, which only created more pain and suffering. Witnessing the blast of negative energy ripped at my heart a little bit that day, as well, if I am being perfectly honest.

This is the trouble with combat or any capital 'T' traumatic event and the mental or spiritual wounding they cause. Trauma can create deep and visceral pain (disturbances to their state of consciousness) that can get stored very deep within the mind and body if one does not have the cognitive tools to process and release it. The senior Marine, by yelling and screaming, purged out his pain because it was so overwhelming. This was necessary for the senior Marine and better than the alternative. Unfortunately, he released this pain (negative energy) onto another human.

It is the storing of the traumatic events in the mind and body that creates the trauma. One of the key themes in the book *The Body Keeps the Score* is "One must remove the stored trauma in order to have any lasting or meaningful healing."

I didn't fully understand the importance of purging as a release mechanism for trauma until many years later, when I met the purgative power of ayahuasca, which I will discuss in detail in Section II.

15

MARRIAGE AND BLOCKED MEMORIES

A good spouse is a mirror that sees what the other cannot. Sometimes, neither can articulate what the other sees, or what may seem inaccurate due to lost memories or protector parts of themselves.

For many years of my marriage, my wife would tell me she thought I had PTSD. I would tell her I absolutely did not have PTSD because I didn't have any event that was overwhelming. Yeah, I had seen or been privy to many traumatic events from my childhood and actions in war. Still, none of those events had broken me. I could talk about these memories and even joke about how screwed up they were. They did not create visceral hatred, nightmares, or panic attacks. So how could I have PTSD?

What neither of us realized at the time was that I had completely blocked and dissociated from my early memories. I had Complex PTSD. CPTSD is quite different than classical or single-event PTSD. It comes from repeated, small (yet meaningful) traumas that make one fear for their lives, not in an overwhelmingly or overly powerful way like an aggravated assault and rape can, or an IED attack while delivering supplies along a supply route will. Complex PTSD is the death by a thousand cuts to the mind. Small, daily, repeated stress fractures to the mind that never seem to end, that one does not have the tools to cognitively process or the power to overcome. Complex PTSD caused me to lock away those memories and feelings and become hypervigilant to the world around me. This hypervigilance led me to pay close attention to my mistakes and those of others, which helped me outperform my peers. It also created a blind spot in my understanding of who I had become, because if I had paid attention to everything, how could I not have seen what my wife saw?

For me, my Complex PTSD was a double-edged sword. On the one hand, it gave me a competitive advantage and greatly reduced the mistakes I made later in life. Conversely, it hid from me very important life moments that made me who I am. This hidden side of me caused me to be emotionally closed off and prevented close relationships with others due to the fear of others, which was imprinted upon me.

The problem with my version of Complex PTSD at such an early age was that it locked in the feeling of loneliness, inadequacy, and unworthiness! It closed off my heart and prevented me from creating and maintaining any deeply meaningful relationships, including my family. On one hand, it was the engine that drove me. On the other hand, it constantly berated me for every mistake I made, making me standoffish and socially withdrawn. My Complex PTSD constantly told me, *How can you be so fucking stupid? How did you not see this coming?*

This internal verbal beratement made me unable to love myself, which, in turn, made it very difficult for others to love me, too.

My wife would often say, "You are a hard person to love."

She was right; I was a hard person to love. I didn't even love myself, so how could someone else love me? Unfortunately, these remarks also reinforced my already-held belief that I was unworthy of love. This is one of the negative side effects of significant trauma during the developmental period of a child's life. As they say, the first five years of a child's development are the most important. Now that I have unlocked the repressed memories and processed much of my early youth, I truly understand how important the first five years are to a person's emotional well-being.

Shortly after returning from Iraq the first time, I went into my four-year-old son's bedroom to get him up and begin the day. As I pulled the sheets off him, I saw that he had wet the bed. Immediately, rage welled up inside me and triggered something inside me that I had never felt before. I completely lost my shit. I screamed at him and began to spank him with anger, just as my father had done to me so many times when I was a small child.

Fortunately, my wife ran into the room and yelled at me to stop. She made me leave, as she (rightfully) held and properly cared for my son. I left the house in an emotional state, which frankly scared me as I walked around the park near our house.

What the fuck did I just do? What the fuck just came over me?

I was mortified. Inside, my heart and soul were crying for my son and berating myself for my actions. Externally, I would not let my tears come to the surface because, in my emotionally disturbed mind, that would be weakness. I had no idea where this unbridled anger came from; I had no idea why I severely overreacted because I had locked away those memories and hid them even from myself.

It wasn't until I was fifty-four years old and only after I unlocked my memory of being ripped from my bed and beaten when I was three that I was able to piece together *why* this happened. Shortly after this revelation in November 2023, I texted my estranged wife what I had learned.

Her immediate answer: "Did you really cry? I've never seen you cry."

OUCH!

She was right, though. She had never seen me cry because I had never trusted her or anyone enough to cry in front of them, and I rarely allowed myself to shed a tear in private. I locked away this very important aspect of healing at a very young age. I was so good at this poor coping mechanism that I could almost always muster the strength to repress and hold the tears down so they never spilled out.

Because I disassociated from my early childhood beatings and never processed those feelings, I was triggered just like my father had been, and did a lesser version to my own child that had been done to me. . . so many times. In my mind, this was a part of me that seemed to come out of nowhere. My behavior shocked me as much as it angered my wife. Subsequently, I spent considerable time berating myself and beating myself up, repeatedly, for how I treated my son, whom I love deeply. It caused me to white-knuckle any future punishment I inflicted on my son. I had to white-knuckle my anger because I had not resolved its source. Hell, at the time, I didn't even remember that any of this had happened to my younger self. All I knew was that I had to make sure that this never happened again!

Luckily, my amazing wife found a great solution: The Naughty Mat. Instead of spanking my son with rage like my father did to me, we placed our son on The Naughty Mat for as many minutes as he was old.

"Sorry, buddy, you have to spend five minutes on The Naughty Mat."

I didn't believe it could work, but I was absolutely willing to give it a try because it kept that raging monster hidden inside me, kept it from unleashing on the child I loved. He hated it, and I loved that I could avoid a situation that risked triggering me into that dark, angry place.

Luckily, it worked! I am so, so grateful for my wife's strength to do what my mom couldn't do for me. By finding a workable alternative to spanking my child with anger, she helped me to break the cycle of generational trauma. She is an amazing mom who deserves a million hugs from a million people.

What I have learned is that feelings and pain cannot be repressed and shoved down, never to be seen again. Emotions have an amazing way of popping up and resurfacing like a cork under water, sometimes at the least expected times. Sometimes, as is the case with people with repressed memories or with Complex PTSD, they manifest in ways that do not make sense at the time. When they do resurface, they reinforce the negative feelings about ourselves that we are ashamed to admit. So, what do we typically do? Shove them down harder, and/or we numb ourselves with alcohol, opioids, or whatever our drug of choice may be.

Repression is a strategy of checking out, whereas one needs to check in with these emotions and process them so that they do not eventually control our lives . . . as they did for me. This is where psychedelic medicine (among other modalities such as EMDR and other forms of therapy) has the power to help reregulate our emotional responses. They provide the tools or a pathway to reconnect to the repressed subconscious and a channel to release. By getting my memories back, I could begin to process them, thus releasing the grip they held on me.

I did to my child exactly as my father had done to me so many times because I had not properly processed these early disturbances in my consciousness that happened so very long ago. The beauty of my version of complex trauma is that it has allowed me to better handle what couldn't be understood or controlled by my three-year-old brain at the time. This distance was created through disassociation. The problem with my disassociation is that it prevented me from resolving the initial traumatic event. Had my wife not been there or had she not been strong enough to address my bad behavior properly, I, too, would have unwittingly passed on my Complex PTSD or unresolved trauma to my own son, given enough time and the right conditions.

We can't fix what we can't remember, or we can't control.

This I Know!

16

HIGH-TEMPO OVERSEAS TOUR

Staying busy can be healthy, or it can prevent revisiting or resolving aspects of your past that you don't want to examine. Busy people are sometimes traumatized people.

After returning from my second and final tour to Iraq, I was assigned a staff job overseas and moved my family to Okinawa, Japan. The job I was slated to fill did not require any travel or deployments, so I thought my family and I would get some really good time together. Unfortunately, due to the Marine Corps needs, the job I was slated for changed. I was shifted to a position that required me to travel off-island, away from my family, and throughout the Pacific for almost 2 of the 3 years we lived in Japan.

I was in charge of the amphibious Navy's future operations team for the forces assigned to Japan. We coordinated the movement and operations of the Navy and Marine Corps Expeditionary forces throughout the Pacific. Our team would deploy to Korea, the Philippines, Australia, Thailand, and India to coordinate military operations with the host countries. A lot of what we did was peacekeeping, humanitarian, or infrastructure-building missions. We conducted three real-world humanitarian assistance and disaster relief missions during my time in

Japan, including support to Taiwan following mudslides and to Indonesia and Japan following earthquakes. We were not doing the killing. We were not causing the destruction. We cooperated with the people in these countries, which made this position rewarding.

My job was extremely professionally rewarding because I was able to get to know people from very different ethnic, religious, and cultural backgrounds than mine, as I broke bread and drank with them. I met some amazing people from Thailand, India, Korea, and other countries; they helped me realize that, despite our cultural and religious differences, we essentially wanted the same things in life. We wanted a safe environment for our family and friends. We wanted a good meal to share with them. We wanted peace with basic rights for everyone we knew.

This extremely busy and rewarding job kept me and my mind actively engaged in the present and future, as it was our responsibility to make sure everything was in place for future multilateral military operations. Because of the high tempo of this job, it satisfied my need to stay busy and avoid the repressed emotions and memories of my past. This high-tempo job kept my mind busy and prevented me from reconnecting with my family, further reinforcing the separation my wife felt from me.

My schedule was always changing with new missions and deployments, causing me to leave my family on short notice. This, of course, reinforced my wife's belief that I could not be counted on and that family was not my priority. Anytime I tried to deflect from the pain of leaving my family. I would state that this was not the job I signed up for and that I intended to be with family and on the island.

She would jokingly respond with, "It may be good for your Korean or Thai family, but it is not good for your American family!"

This created constant tension between us, as I knew she was right. I was angry at myself for failing my family. Every time we argued, I would defend what I was powerless to control while, at the same time, berating myself for being so stupid or naive to think that moving my family halfway around the world was a good idea. By the end of the three-year tour, my wife and I were no closer, and her bitterness toward me was palpable.

A few months before the tour ended, the largest earthquake in recorded history struck mainland Japan. The earthquake triggered a large tsunami, creating a humanitarian and radiological crisis. I immediately deployed to Yokota, Japan, with my planning team to lead the U.S. Navy's response, which canceled our family trip to tour Japan on the way back to the U.S.

Shortly after arriving in Yokota, it became apparent that the command initially put in charge (US Forces Japan) was neither manned nor had the experience to command such a large operation. They were a staff command focused on political and military relations who arranged for diplomatic clearances, not for running multiservice complex operations.

Since I had spent the last three years traveling around Asia working with all the operators, I was familiar with the people and their capabilities, so I moved my way up to the lead future operations planner for the entire operation. In this position, I would routinely brief senior leadership (Generals and Admirals). As we were wrapping up operations, a couple of the Marine Generals asked what was next for me and whether they could do anything to help me in my career. I let them know that I was leaving the Marine Corps after my next and last tour. I knew my wife and family needed me around, and any position that would ensure promotion would be another tour like the present one: good for the career, but bad for the marriage and family.

17

TWILIGHT TOUR

The last military job a person has prior to leaving service. It is meant to facilitate an easier transition to civilian life and a less stressful environment.

Upon returning to the United States after Okinawa, I was stationed at Scott Air Force Base just outside of St. Louis, Missouri. I knew this was my last tour before retirement because I made a promise to my wife many years prior. I told her that if she would allow me to stay for 20 years so I could receive a pension, then she could opt out at any time after that. When it came time to make this decision, for obvious reasons, she wanted out!! She immediately chose to leave and wanted to return to our once-shared hometown.

This meant I needed to focus on adapting my skills and language for reentering civilian life. I applied to and was blessed and grateful to be accepted to a top-tier MBA program at the Olin Business School at Washington University in St. Louis. This was my ticket to transition away from anything military-related and to start a fresh new chapter in corporate America . . . or so I thought.

In the School of Business, I found highly successful people who spoke a seemingly different language and who were motivated by titles, position, and money. They were connected and respected, and many were being groomed for senior leadership positions within their company. I was taken aback by how much they valued profit and not people.

One day, fairly early in the program, our class was discussing something like Internal Rate of Return (IRR) vs. Return On Investment (ROI), or something along those lines. When I announced to the whole class, "I worked in a currency much more valuable than the U.S. dollar," many of my classmates looked at me as though I were crazy. In their minds, there is nothing more valuable than the U.S. dollar. After all, it is the global reserve currency. I then told them that the currency I worked in was human lives, and that we need to consider the lives affected by these financial decisions.

I could tell many of my classmates either didn't get it or felt uncomfortable around me . . . I didn't care. I had spoken up against what I felt was their arrogance and ignorance. It is my opinion that this corporate focus on profits over people is what has significantly contributed to the decline of the middle class and the large increase in the unhoused populations in the U.S.

I also realized I was different and needed to adapt and modify my language if I ever hoped to assimilate back into 'normal' corporate society. I worked hard to adapt, and I performed well. I graduated in the top half, even though I was only publicly educated and did not grow up in St. Louis, so I did not understand or fit into the rules of the game.

After graduating from WashU with an MBA and for the year prior to exiting the Marine Corps, I applied for hundreds of jobs in the private sector. I applied for anything that didn't have a connection to the military because I wanted to close the chapter on everything military-related. Because I was trying to step so far out of my military experience, I received almost no interviews. Either I was overqualified, older than they were looking for, or lacked the industry experience to be competitive for jobs at my skill level. In other words, I didn't fit into what corporate America wanted, nor could I seem to get past the Human Resources gatekeepers. So, I gave up trying to penetrate corporate America. Additionally, if I am being perfectly honest, I was also hamstrung by my Complex PTSD, which prevented me from creating meaningful connections with my peers. I was different, and I knew it.

Luckily, as a Marine operator accustomed to working in austere, unpredictable environments, I pivoted and adapted to entrepreneurship. After I retired from the military, like many, I moved back to my hometown and returned to what I knew before joining—construction and real estate. As a child, I spent all my summers working for my father. My father had been an architect, builder, and small developer for whom I worked during most of my youth.

In fact, as a small child, I would routinely be asked for my name by the building inspectors as they toured the job sites where I was working. It wasn't until later in life that I realized why they asked and that there are child labor laws that prevent this type of labor. Because I was family, these laws had no jurisdiction over me. After my father's death, my siblings and I were fortunate to inherit a couple of buildings he owned. I was elected to run them for my brother and sister because I was the only family member who could be trusted with the assets. So, I leaned back into this industry armed with my military experience and recently acquired MBA.

I want to reiterate that I understand how blessed I am to have had this skill and opportunity as a fallback. Many of my military brothers and sisters are not so lucky. When they return home, their military experience doesn't quite fit the mold of society, so they struggle to fit back in. Too many returning veterans can't make the transition back into 'normal' civilian society. The challenges veterans face become two-fold when reentering society. They are no longer a good fit in their communities, and they may have been exposed to traumatic events that they have not yet fully processed. These two aspects are what alienate our military upon leaving the service.

Too many returning veterans spiral downward, becoming lost, unproductive, and eventually unhoused. Too many take their own lives. The invisible stress fractures in their minds begin to expand and eat away at their perceived value when they have the time to 'sit in' these thoughts. Even though I was blessed to have a fallback, I fell down this same path.

18

AFTER RETIREMENT

Without Purpose: Life does not seem to go as well

Military service gives one a rank, a role, and a responsibility to oneself and to others. It creates a sense of purpose in life, which keeps the mind, body, and spirit healthy and whole. Many who leave the military begin to lose their identity, pride, productivity, and hope. The challenges of leaving military service, coupled with unresolved aspects of their service, can make conditions ripe for this loss of self and purpose.

Reflecting on one's actions or inaction during war, training accidents, or other significant stressors can be the catalyst for a downward spiral. Many do not understand what they feel or why they feel the way they do. They lack the cognitive tools to address their trauma, are too proud to seek help, or believe they are being weak. Instead of asking for help, many begin to close down. How do I know this? I know this because I started to do the same when I was back in my hometown. I never signed up or sought Veterans Administration (VA) care because the veterans I knew who were using their mental health services were not satisfied.

The VA is currently legally hamstrung from helping these individuals. I know of too many veterans who have sought help, only to be given prescription drugs that mask the problem instead of resolving the underlying cause. The VA recognizes this shortfall, which is why they are heavily investing in psychedelic research. Unfortunately, due to current laws, they are unable to use the tool, which has the greatest potential positive impact on many returning veterans, including myself.

It was a long, slippery slope that slowly crept up on me and into my life over several years. I found myself back in the town where I had grown up, which was once familiar but now felt foreign. It was still a smallish midwestern town with its local, small-town viewpoint. I had spent my adult life far away, involved in national and global problems. My view and interest in the world were so different from those of the people I now lived and worked among. I struggled to find meaning and purpose after I returned.

In my previous life, I was the lead planner and architect of the US military's supporting plan for the 2011 tsunami and radiological crisis. In this role, I personally briefed the Joint Chairman of the Japanese Self-Defense Force (JSDF) on US support for Japan's humanitarian and radiological crisis. I had gone from being a global strategic planner coordinating multimillion dollar operations throughout the Pacific. Now, a few years later, I was back in my hometown trying to establish a new life and a new profession. In this pursuit, I couldn't even seem to get subcontractors to show up for work, and I had no power to make them because I had no recourse. I was a nobody in this world because I was new. To be honest, it was quite the fall. It was frustrating for me, who had significant power and respect in the military, to come back to my hometown and be a nobody. These frustrations grew into anger, which spilled out onto my wife and family.

My emotional unavailability and anger were driving my wife away and causing her to cope in the same way my mom chose—alcohol. My wife began to drink heavily as she turned away from me, as I became too much for her to deal with.

For me, being back in the hometown I never wanted to return to, along with my wife's drinking, triggered unresolved aspects of my past. I still hadn't fully reconciled or processed my own mother's death due to alcoholism, and I couldn't handle witnessing my wife, whom I loved very much, do the same. Over the next few years, I slowly watched my wife drift away and witness alcohol start to take her down the same path my mother chose. All of this ignited my Complex PTSD.

With my Complex PTSD triggered, and my wife's behavior destructive, our relationship began the downward spiral, which only triggered and reinforced each other's destructive (wounded) behaviors. As I was now forced to sit in what I thought I had left behind so very long ago, my repressed emotions started to express themselves in unhealthy ways that caused my loved ones to distance themselves from me. This, in turn, created an emotional isolation within me, which caused my anger to spill out. Unfortunately, this emotional 'man-cave' further reinforced my emotional unavailability, which drove my wife's actions to begin with. In other words, each of our actions made the other not feel safe in their environment. It became the death spiral for our relationship.

In May 2020, just after COVID hit, my wife moved out, and we became separated. Looking back, this was the best thing for both of us because we became each other's source of pain/triggers. We both needed a safe place to live so that we could begin the healing process individually.

After my wife and I separated, I felt stuck and angry—angry that even though I never hit my wife, nor spanked any of my children with anger, except that one time, that somehow, I found myself in a very similar situation to that of my parents prior to their deaths. How is it that I did everything in my power to escape my past, only to be facing the similar stresses and pains my parents felt?

I had done everything in my power to separate myself and those I loved from the traumatic things I had to endure as a child, just like my dad did with how he perceived the brutal dysfunctions of his family upbringing.

My father thought being poor was what caused all their pain and suffering. This is why he worked really, really hard to ensure that a lack of money would not be the root of his family's problems. We both did the best we could, with what we knew, but because neither of us had fully and properly processed these early experiences and learned their lessons, I was destined to repeat the generational pattern of anger and emotional unavailability that my father had unwittingly taught me.

The woman I loved was drinking to escape just like my mother had done because I had become my father in a couple of key ways. As I sat in my own anger and beratement of myself, I began to realize that I had a hoarder's basement of stuffed and repressed emotions that I couldn't seem to shove any more into.

I was full!

There was no more room to put anything ANYWHERE. As I tried to shove something in, something else would spill out. I was trying so hard not to let anything spill out, but was failing. I was drowning in unresolved emotional pain. I found myself in a very similar position to my father's twenty-plus years earlier. Like him, I was having to deal with a lifetime of suppressed or repressed emotions that seemed to be flooding into my consciousness and were interfering with my ability to be productive. Once my anger began spilling over onto my adult children, I knew I had to do something, otherwise I was going to choose the same path that brought my own father to hit the reset button in this game we call life.

It was my love for my children and the promise that I made to myself so very long ago that forced me to search for another way out. After my dad took his own life and as I walked away from his funeral, I made a promise to myself that I would never do what he did because I understood the pain that it created for those left behind.

The problem with this promise to myself was that, at this point in my life, I had no love or even care for myself. My internal, extremely critical 'Voice of Beratement' was becoming more active and ever-present in my life. It was berating me for not showing up in life; it was berating me for most of my days and most of my actions. It was becoming overwhelming and was overtaking me as I was losing my separation from its hurtful and hateful tone. This internal 'Voice of Beratement' was putting me in the death spiral, and I was circling the drain. I kept telling myself that suicide wasn't an acceptable option for me, but I was oh so ready to get off this Wheel of Pain we call life.

Some call this moment 'the dark night of the soul.' I can tell you that what I experienced was dark, heavy, and crushing at the time! I found myself, once again, in a dark and severe thunderstorm that was bouncing me around to where I felt alone and I had lost control, only this time, a part of me wanted to die.

Luckily, I found another path: a medicinal release valve that helped me to resolve the anger and abuse within, to confront the trauma and sadness that I tightly held onto—and that held onto me. With the help of this medicine, I was able to clean out my hoarder's basement of repressed emotions, fear, and pain.

In this process, I found the super-cute, adorable three-year-old version of myself, locked in a back room of my hoarder's basement full of lost memories. This medicine gave me the key to free this abused child who had been imprisoned for fifty years, and I was able to find the compassion and forgiveness for myself that my father couldn't seem to find. For the grace of God, I was given the opportunity to resolve my disturbances and conflicts within through the proper use of psilocybin, MDMA, and ayahuasca.

I WILL BE FOREVER GRATEFUL!!!

The next section of this memoir takes you through this journey!

SECTION II

TRANSFORMATION

A profound and deliberate process of change involving a significant shift in one's understanding of oneself or the world.

Before my transformation and in the summer of 2020, my wife and I separated because my emotional unavailability and anger toward her excessive alcohol consumption were reinforcing each other's bad behaviors, thus becoming an untenable position for either of us. She was drinking to mask her pain just like my mother had. At this point, I had not resolved the disturbances from my childhood, early adult life, and from watching my mother drink herself to death: I felt I was now witnessing the same pattern with my wife, and to put it bluntly, it pissed me off. As I settled into this new reality of living alone, I realized I had a lot of emotional unpacking to do.

This Section contains details regarding my personal use of psilocybin, MDMA, and ayahuasca under therapeutic protocols. I was desperate for relief from the mental pain that my unprocessed negative life experiences were causing me. My actions, at the time, were illegal in the United States, and I fully understood this before utilizing these medicines to help me understand and resolve my past traumas.

Unfortunately, psilocybin has been illegal in the United States since Richard Nixon signed the Controlled Substances Act in 1970, and MDMA was added to the Schedule I drug list in 1985 due to backlash from the rave culture. For the last four to five decades, these medicines have been classified as Schedule I drugs, which means they are substances with a high potential for abuse and no currently accepted medical use. Recent clinical trials are showing that psychedelic drugs actually have a very low potential for abuse and can be very effective in treating depression, anxiety, trauma, and other mental health-related issues.

What I have learned through research and personal experience is that psychedelics can be a form of medicine and are a viable treatment for serious mental health conditions such as Complex PTSD, which hopefully my story will adequately outline. Psychedelic medicines have helped me change my life in such a profound and positive way.

For the record, I am not a psychonaut or a regular user of these drugs/medicines. As of this publication, I have done a combination of MDMA and psilocybin four times total. I have not had a need, want, or desire to take MDMA since my birthday on October 28th, 2023. I have found great benefit from the few times I have taken them, and (currently) I am really good at just loving and integrating everything they have taught and continue to teach me.

Additionally, I attended the Multidisciplinary Approach to Psychedelic Studies (MAPS.org) biennial psychedelic conference in the summer of 2025, where I attended with over 9,000 global participants. At the conference, I attended workshops and held discussions with trained psychiatrists who have been involved in recent U.S. clinical trials. I wanted to ensure I had the most up-to-date information and was not misinforming as I told my story.

While I tout the wonders of psychedelics as a viable mental health treatment modality, I used many other modalities during my transformation journey. These modalities included psychotherapy with EMDR, breathwork, meditation, and physical exercise, including yoga and backpacking, as means to help me integrate what my psychedelic experiences revealed to me. In other words, less radical treatment solutions are proving successful now that the major memory blockages and dysregulations have been cleared. As I have mentioned previously, *you cannot resolve what you can't remember or control!*

I am onc of the most blessed individuals in this world, because God (god)/spirit/universe took care of me as I journeyed inward to understand myself. Additionally, if I am being honest, I took care of myself as well. The transformation story I am about to tell will (hopefully) adequately convey what I have learned, which is that *psychedelic medicine under proper protocols has the power to re-regulate your emotional default mode network into a calmer and less hypervigilant or stressed homeostasis.*

This I Know!

19

SAFETY IS AT THE ROOT OF HEALING

Feeling safe, both physically and emotionally, is fundamental for healing from trauma, stress, or any challenging experience. It's not just a feeling but a physiological state that allows the body and mind to shift from survival mode into repair and growth.

As I begin to tell my transformation story, I want to briefly discuss how recent clinical trials are using psychedelics to treat trauma patients so that a baseline of understanding can be shared by us both. I was blessed to accidentally stumble into the proper therapeutic protocols, which is what made these compounds so effective for me. I can attest to the importance of these key factors I describe below.

Trauma is fear that gets encoded in our bodies. If the trauma or fear response manifests far enough out in the emotional regulatory response spectrum, it can manifest as Post Traumatic Stress Disorder/Dysregulation (PTSD), as it did for me.

To unwind this subconscious activation and behavior, the psychiatrist, psychedelic-trained therapist, shaman, or other qualified person must place the traumatized person into a physically and mentally safe environment. Safety is at the root of healing because we cannot heal unless we feel safe. Our recovery repair network shuts down in the presence of stress or threat.

Modern life is filled with constant stressors that flood the body with stress response hormones such as cortisol and adrenaline, as well as other emotional neurotransmitters, keeping the individual on the sympathetic side of the autonomic nervous system, or 'on alert.' When the body is on the sympathetic side, which is the fight or flight side, higher cognitive thinking and the body's natural ability to heal are tuned down or shut off completely when the stress response becomes high enough: panic! So, for many, the modern mind struggles to feel safe enough to repair itself.

If the stress or threat can be removed for long enough and under the right conditions, as I did, this will allow our bodies' natural healing mechanisms to work, including mental health! The challenge for those who have PTSD, like me, is that it takes extreme safety in order to overcome the extreme fear that caused their emotional dysregulation to begin with. With this in mind, safety is the foundation for allowing these medicines to work, and the key components of safety are SET AND SETTING.

Your *mindSET* means you need to genuinely want to resolve the underlying emotional or mental distress without fear, judgment, or other protective coping mechanisms interfering with your journey into resolving your past. If you are afraid of going in or facing your past, then your mind will diminish the effectiveness of these medications. I truly did not know the answers to my questions, and I was honestly curious about them.

The right *Setting* is your surrounding environment. The environment needs to be one with no perceived threats or aspects that would put you on alert. In other words, you must be in an environment that feels both physically and mentally safe. The environment cannot trigger or activate your 'protector parts,' which push your emotional autonomic nervous system into the sympathetic side, thus limiting your brain and your body's natural ability to heal.

With an internal and external safe environment in place, one must ask the right question (*INTENTION*) and allow and hold the space for what you are shown during the journey (*INTEGRATION*). It is your intention that focuses your mind on where to begin your journey inward. If what you are trying to examine, thus resolve, is not fully understood or you have protective parts which prevent examination, then psychedelic medicines in low to medium doses may not be able to resolve. To bypass these coping mechanisms, larger doses of psychedelic medicine or ones that have a dissociative effect could be required. They do this by taking parts of your brain offline or stimulating parts that are tuned down. This is why choosing the right medicine in the proper dosage and receiving professional care are critical for success.

As I discovered, your intention is very important to your success. Your Intention needs to be authentic and genuine; otherwise, parts of you will prevent the journey inward (IFS protector parts). To go into your past, you must seek out the past distress with a calm mind and curiosity, so that no matter what the journey shows you, you can radically accept or have *compassion* for whatever comes up.

What I have learned through multiple journeys with different medicines is that the psychiatrist, mental health practitioner, or trip sitter's two main responsibilities are to provide a safe container and help to establish the intention. They establish the safe container by putting the patient in an emotional and physical state of trust. They can also assist the patient in choosing an intention that touches on aspects they do not understand and want to take in, or that they need help letting go of. This intention should be stated aloud when taking the medicine.

With these aspects in place, the patient, like me, can relax enough and have enough guidance to allow the medicine and their own natural healing mechanisms to work. During the journey, when the patient is under the medicine, the clinician acts as a caring facilitator, not a problem solver, unless specifically asked, and the person under the medicine is in a state of *clarity*. Often, it is best to delay any conversation until the journey is over, so the patient/person can continue to explore what is being shown. It is during the post-experience integrative sessions that your skills and insight as a mental health professional or caring person are most important.

My experiences have taught me that the *set*, *setting*, *intention*, and *integration* are as important as the medicine itself, if not more so! The medicine does not do the work for you, but connects you back with yourself or what you already know but have hidden from yourself; they are catalysts for each other! Through proper regulation and psychiatric safety protocols, the risks involved are greatly reduced. I can tell you from personal experience that some of these journeys can be extremely difficult, so having people around you who can ensure your safety is very important. This is why I advocate for the psychedelic-assisted psychotherapy or trip-sitter model versus unregulated or recreational use of these powerful medicinal drugs.

That said, I want to convey that I have tremendous empathy for those who need the relief these medicines provide but do not have the financial means or personal flexibility to travel to other countries to find it; hence, one of the reasons I wrote this memoir. After all, if I waited for legalization in the U.S., I would still be mentally unhealthy and circling the drain. Worse yet, I would be another veteran statistic regarding suicide. My transformation story would never have had an opportunity to be told. I was desperate for a solution that the U.S. legal system did not allow for. I know I am not alone in this need.

Because these medicines are so powerful, they must be taken with the utmost respect and reverence. It is when they are not administered and taken with the proper mindset, in a safe environment, and with plans to mitigate any difficulties that can and do arise that negative outcomes can occur. If a person has a chaotic or angry mindset or perceives the setting as unsafe, this is how 'bad' trips can occur. These negative consequences can be avoided if proper safety protocols and reverence and respect for the medicines are put in place.

This I Know!

20

CHANGING MY CLOSED MIND

Your mindset is the attitude, fundamental set of beliefs, and perspectives that shape how you handle challenges and view the world. A closed mind creates barriers and limitations in life that limit your full potential and happiness. Open your mind, and the rest will follow.

In 2019, prior to my separation from my wife, we watched the movie *Fantastic Fungi*, which discusses the importance of mushrooms to our ecosystem; fungi are instrumental in breaking down materials and making them biologically available for regeneration. The documentary gave me a new appreciation for the regenerative power of mushrooms.

I was particularly fascinated with the main character, Paul Stamet, and his experience with psychedelic mushrooms as a youth. As an aside to the main story, Paul mentioned that he had a stutter as a child. As a young teenager, he ingested a large dose of psychedelic mushrooms. Under their effects, he was able to will himself to stop stuttering. To me, this was an interesting story, but it didn't seem relevant to my life, so I didn't give it much thought. Little did I know that, in the near future, psychedelic mushrooms would be the 'gateway drug' that would facilitate my journey into finding who I had become and why. While the movie did not get me curious enough to use psychedelic mushrooms, it did, however, begin to open my mind to their potential benefits.

Before my transformation, my formula of aviate, navigate, and communicate was breaking down to the point that I wasn't doing well communicating what I was feeling because I didn't understand much about my emotions or why my autonomic nervous system was always in a heightened, overactive state. I was finding out that you can repress or set aside unresolved emotionally negative events and the imprinting these experiences have on your subconscious for only so long. I had stacked up a lifetime of traumatic events, which started to reenter my life despite my desire and effort to deny and keep pushed down and away.

Additionally, I was beginning to realize that my lack of purpose and being back in the hometown where I grew up were allowing space for old, repressed wounds to resurface. All the family dysfunction that I had left behind 21 years ago—that I thought I had moved past—began to reenter my life.

People I knew on the outside periphery, friends of friends, who had troubled pasts, were talking about microdosing mushrooms and stating they were having success. Microdosing, what is that? Based upon what these people were saying, microdosing seemed much less scary than consuming a heroic dose, which Paul Stamot took when he willed himself to stop stuttering as a youth.

Over the months in the latter half of 2020 and the first half of 2021, I talked to various people and learned that you do not 'trip.' In fact, you probably won't feel any different if they are taken properly and in low enough doses. They do not alter your reality, but just calm the mind and body enough to stay in the present.

Learning that I will always be in control and that the world does not shift around me soothed the 'protector parts' of my mind. As a person who needed to be in control and came from a family where drugs had caused my dog's death, and had slowly ended my mom's life, I was keenly aware of the dangers of drugs. Additionally, it was my ability to stay away from drugs as a youth that created my successes. Microdosing psilocybin seemed like a way to gently crack open the door to this world without a fear of breaking the door off its hinges.

I now understand that microdosing mushrooms on a daily or routine basis is like taking any other medication daily. People who take Selective Serotonin Reuptake Inhibitors (SSRIs) for depression are, in essence, microdosing the antidepressant on a daily basis. However, the mechanisms these two medicines use to control serotonin are opposing.

SSRIs work by preventing the reuptake of serotonin, thereby increasing the amount of bioavailable serotonin at the synapse. Psilocybin, on the other hand, breaks down into psilocin. Psilocin binds and activates the 5-HT2(A-C) serotonin receptors in the brain. This, in turn, makes the receptors more active, allowing the existing serotonin levels to be more readily available.

Additionally, due to its neuroplastic effects, psilocin alters brain activity, reducing default mode network (DMN) activity and increasing connectivity between brain regions. All of which allow for the person to form new thought processes or perceptions. *Recent clinical trials and loosened regulations in Oregon and Colorado are showing that when you combine psilocybin mushrooms with cognitive-behavioral therapy or deep self-reflection, the neuroplastic effects can yield more meaningful, longer-lasting cognitive-behavioral outcomes.*

SSRIs address the symptom of low serotonin bioavailability by increasing serotonin levels. This serves to mask the underlying dysregulation, but once the medication is out of the system, it reemerges. This is why people need to be on SSRIs long term and why, when they try to get off the medicine, their problems typically return.

Psilocin, on the other hand, addresses the underlying receptor efficiency by increasing its efficiency. They do this by stimulating 5-HT2A receptors, which promote the formation of new dendrites. This process, called synaptogenesis, increases the body's serotonin efficiency, which, in essence, reduces emotional dysregulation. This is a part of the complex neuroplastic effect that psychedelic medicines offer, thus contributing to a greater long-term solution without the need for constant medication. They can help facilitate a rebalancing of the nervous system by reducing the underlying dysregulation.

I have since learned that psilocybin, as well as ayahuasca, is not compatible with SSRIs. Psilocybin/psilocin preserves or enhances emotional neurological responsiveness, whereas SSRIs can cause emotional blunting. Because they work from opposing mechanisms, SSRIs can reduce the effectiveness of psilocybin. When taken together, they can have some harmful side effects, such as serotonin toxicity. If you are taking SSRIs like Zoloft or Prozac, do not consider taking psilocybin mushrooms or ayahuasca until you have been off of SSRIs for a considerable period (one month or more if you have been on an SSRI for any considerable period). Please consult a healthcare provider if you are currently or have recently been on SSRIs.

I have never taken an SSRI, so my direct knowledge is lacking. A crude, maybe oversimplistic, explanation based upon my discussion with professionals and reading professional papers is that SSRIs numb you from yourself. In contrast, psychedelics like psilocybin and ayahuasca connect you back to yourself. This is where the trouble begins: the two medicines are pushing in opposite directions. One cannot have a transformative experience or journey when they are disconnected or blunted from themselves.

As a child of generational trauma, who used the coping mechanism of disassociation to the point I was circling the drain, I can say that it was my reconnection to myself that created the conditions for the transformational experience. *You have to go in and go through . . . in order to get out!*

This I Know!

21

DIPPING MY TOE INTO PSYCHEDELICS

Starting slowly and deliberately to ensure success requires education and measured implementation to mitigate unknown risks.

In the summer of 2021, my introspective journey into understanding who I had become began in earnest. On a nice late summer Sunday around noon, I decided to dip my toe into the waters of microdosing psilocybin mushrooms. I obtained a few grams of psilocybin mushrooms. From what I had learned from others and confirmed with a simple internet search, I was only supposed to take between .1 and .3 grams. So, I broke off a small section of a stem (~.1 grams) and ate it.

I was a little nervous about its effects, which, looking back, seems extremely naive, but I was dipping my toe into unknown territory. Before I took the mushrooms, I set the intention that I was not going to leave the four corners of my property to ensure I didn't behave inappropriately while out in public. When I took the mushrooms, I told myself, "*Just let the day happen,*" which wasn't very normal of me. Because in my hyperactive mind, I always needed a plan or a mental list of things I wanted to accomplish in the day. In other words, I did not set any expectations for how today was going to go, other than setting my boundaries for where I could go. Looking back, I think this lack of resistance helped me achieve my benefits.

Shortly after I took the mushrooms, I checked in with myself. At first, I did not notice that I felt affected in any way. In fact, I was a little disappointed that nothing seemed to be happening to me, aside from a slight stomach uneasiness. So, I went through the day thinking I didn't take enough to have an effect. I did a little cleaning around the house, organized a few piles that had been sitting around, and engaged in a little yard work. I found myself just doing what I wanted, without beating myself up for allowing this work to remain undone before. A few hours later, I decided to lie down on my hammock and relax.

One of the side effects of my hypervigilance was that I couldn't sit still or sit and do nothing for any period. Any time I tried to sit and relax, my voice of beratement would remind me that I was being lazy, and that laziness was not acceptable if I was to *be better.*

As I sat and relaxed in the hammock, I noticed I felt content with what I had accomplished. I was not berating myself for letting the dirty dishes pile up to begin with, or for the piles of clean, unfolded clothes to sit for almost a week. The internal voice that would shame me for relaxing wasn't so present. It was a good, productive day, but I didn't feel as though the mushrooms had done anything, so I wasn't excited to take them again.

About two weeks later, I decided to take a little bit of mushrooms, again, on an early Sunday afternoon. Only this time, I took a little more, approximately 0.2 to 0.3 grams, since I didn't feel much of anything the first time. Again, I had another productive day without feeling like I was on any hallucinogenic drug. After a few hours of yard work, I laid on the hammock and looked around while reflecting on my mowed lawn and my trimmed bushes. As I lay down, I am very present, looking up and observing the tree branches slowly blowing in the wind. I think to myself, "*I feel good*."

Wait . . .

Did I feel good? How is this possible? The chronic pain throughout my body from years of sports, the Marine Corps, and breaking my back fourteen years earlier seemed to be dulled. I also noticed that the colors of the leaves and flower blooms seemed to be a little brighter. I felt a little respite from the constant chatter of the voices in my head, which I later learned was my voice of beratement.

I live on a busy corner of town, where my house sits next to a highway that runs through it. As I lay on my hammock, my mind felt clearer and quieter, as though my mental rush-hour traffic had slowed . . . I felt more present.

I took stock of what I accomplished over the last couple of hours and thought, *"Today has been a lovely day."* 'Lovely day' had not been in my vocabulary for the last several years. I was more present, calm, and felt a little contentment again.

Neuroscientists would explain what I felt was my nervous system shifting from the 'fight or flight' active or sympathetic state to the parasympathetic or relaxed 'rest and digest' state. It was a great day. Could this be the mushrooms? No, it couldn't be the mushrooms because I did not have any hallucinogenic or euphoric drug experience.

Well, of course, my relaxed nervous system was related to the mushrooms; this is how microdosing mushrooms works. Microdosing psilocybin makes one more present, less chaotic or busy in the mind, and more focused on what one wants or needs to do—or at least it does for me.

If you find yourself with ADHD issues or having trouble being present, then I believe microdosing could potentially be of benefit to you as well. Some retrospective surveys indicate that routine microdosing can be as effective, if not more so, than traditional ADHD medicines. I would love to see a clinical trial comparing the two methods to determine which is more effective long-term. Still, research such as this is prohibited under U.S. Schedule I classification.

Microdosing mushrooms these first couple of times introduced to me what a calm, relaxed state of mind feels like . . . something I hadn't felt in a really, really long time. What I didn't realize, until over two years later, was that psilocybin quieted my internal dialogue, which used to yell and berate me for every mistake I made. Microdosing helped me quiet this internal voice, which kept my mind and body on the 'fight or flight' side of my nervous system, keeping me actively on alert. I liked what the mushrooms did for me, but did not want to take drugs regularly, so I didn't take them again for over seven months until late spring of 2022. I wanted to sit with my thoughts about taking mushrooms and to make sure I wouldn't get addicted.

Because I have a brother who has suffered from severe drug addiction since high school and still struggles with addiction, I wanted to make sure that I didn't accidentally fall into the same addiction trap as him. Truthfully, I also had to mentally wrestle with the 1970s and early 1980s war on drugs drumbeat that drugs are evil and can fry your brain.

I still remember the campaign where they showed an egg frying in a pan, with the tagline "This is your brain on drugs." They were so successful in their messaging, coupled with knowing my own success came from turning away from drugs, that it created the mindset that I should avoid drugs at all costs. I was so anti-drug that I rarely took over-the-counter pain medicines unless I really was hurting.

What I have since learned is that psilocybin mushrooms have an extremely low risk for addiction, which runs counter to their drug classification in the U.S. It is the people who use them to mask their mental disturbances instead of facing and processing what is brought up who are most prone to addiction to these substances. They use them to check out rather than check in. The mindset is the most powerful factor in determining the effectiveness of these medicines. If your mind does not want to resolve, then the medicine will not work.

In April 2022, I was doing spring cleaning and came across the mushrooms that I had only taken a couple of times before. I knew they seemed to help, and I never had the feeling, "Where are they?" or that I needed them to function, so I decided to dip my toe back into microdosing. Over the late spring, summer, and fall of 2022, I took a very low dose of mushrooms about a dozen times. Every time I consumed a little bit of the mushrooms, it was on the weekend, and I would turn off my notifications or put my phone away so I wouldn't be distracted. I set the experience up for success by going to the grocery store before consuming and by not leaving the four corners of my property or doing anything related to business while on them. In fact, I never took them after 2 p.m. as I wanted to ensure I had them out of my system by nightfall (for whatever reason).

My home is my sanctuary, and I feel extremely safe and relaxed at home. I have a wonderful yard, which brings me joy to work in. In the spring, summer, and fall, I spend many hours of many days taking care of it. From mowing the lawn to raking leaves, putting down mulch, or trimming the plants and trees, this mindless work is very satisfying to my soul. I love walking barefoot, listening to music, and tuning out the stresses of life.

Gardening is therapeutic for me. Gardening while microdosing mushrooms enhances its therapeutic effect. To be in the present moment of looking at the various leaf and branch patterns and how they interplay throughout the garden . . . the bright pink blossoms, nestled in the chartreuse serrated leaves, next to a deep purple succulent . . . well, you get the picture. By being so in the present, I was able to relax into my thoughts and feelings. This is exactly what I needed as someone who denied or repressed so much.

I like to be out in Mother Nature and ground myself in the earth when I take them. The 7.83 Hz frequency the earth resonates at and its grounding effect seem to enhance my calming experience. Just Google 'grounding and vagus nerve' and you will see that science seems to back up what I intrinsically felt.

I microdose psilocybin to do 'inner work' as a means to *check IN,* not *check OUT.* With a *calmer* nervous system and a quieter mind, deep into self-reflective thought, I was able to uncover unresolved disturbances and old wounds that were still hanging out in my subconscious. Microdosing psilocybin helps me stay present in my thoughts, similar to what meditation is designed to do. It was the safe set and setting, along with my introspective intention, that made them so effective for me.

I use the mushrooms to *calmly* sit in my thoughts rather than avoid them. Microdosing psilocybin calmed my mind enough for me to see and understand how my thoughts were affecting me. Microdosing allowed thoughts to slowly percolate without overwhelming me. The mushrooms quieted the parts of me that created excuses (protector parts) or berated me for previous mistakes. Because I was able to observe and accept whatever was on my mind, I could let it go.

By quieting these critical parts, I was able to find a little more *compassion* for myself. I have always berated myself for simple mistakes. If I can't find my keys, I would mentally abuse myself for being stupid for not remembering where I laid them earlier in the day. I would also beat myself up for not paying attention to something or for being mentally lazy and forgetting basic stuff. I was really good at the complicated, but much of daily life created difficulties for me. In other words, I can be the 'absent-minded professor' type.

When winter and the cold came, I took the last of the mushrooms I had, but did not enjoy the experience nearly as much. Being stuck in the house was not the set or setting that gave me nearly the pleasure that being outside, in nature, mowing the grass, pulling weeds, and trimming bushes did. So, I stopped microdosing over the winter. Instead, I turned my attention to nature documentaries and documentaries in general.

22

EXPANDING MY PERSPECTIVE

Psychedelic Drugs will fry your brain and are as bad as cocaine and methamphetamine . . . or are they?

In January 2023, I came across the Netflix series, *How to Change Your Mind.* The documentary is a four-part series based on the book by Michael Pollan titled the same. Michael Pollan narrates the docuseries and discusses the history of psychedelics and how psychedelics have the potential to treat many human mental health conditions like anxiety, depression, and PTSD.

As someone who was beginning to see the effectiveness of microdosing psilocybin and a military veteran who knew many who had PTSD, I thought the series might be of interest. This documentary did exactly what the title stated. It changed my mind on what these powerful drugs have to offer under the right circumstances and professional guidance. I learned so much about how these powerful medicines can affect brain neuroplasticity and help rewire mental patterns through this mechanism. I highly recommend!

The first episode is on LSD and the 60s culture in the U.S., and discusses the government's action to classify these drugs as a Schedule I drug. A drug classified as Schedule I means it has no accepted medical use, therefore is banned from any use or purpose, including research. The government classified these compounds as such, even though there was significant evidence from the psychiatrists and mental health practitioners that there was significant benefit in the mental health arena. The government banned these powerful medicines due to the hippie culture's embrace, behavior, and rebellion from societal norms. Let this serve as a lesson to both sides of the argument on how to appropriately proceed with rescheduling these compounds as we move forward toward reclassification. The emerging evidence from recent clinical trials overwhelmingly shows that these compounds are scheduled inappropriately in the U.S. My experiences back up what these clinical trials are proving, which is that these compounds have a medical benefit and have a low risk for addiction and abuse.

The second episode of the docuseries is on psychedelic or 'magic' mushrooms and psilocybin. This episode does a great job of explaining how these powerful medicines work in the mind. I was very intrigued by other people's stories and how they seemed to match my recent, yet limited, microdosing experiences to some degree. However, the episode's main focus was on much larger dosages with much more dramatic results.

Psilocybin mushrooms can be very gentle when utilized in microdoses (0.1–0.3 grams), or they can hit you hard if taken in much larger quantities, such as a heroic dose (5+ grams). An analogy that I resonate with is comparing psilocybin mushrooms to hammering a nail into a piece of wood. If the person microdoses psilocybin, they are hitting the nail with a tiny hammer, with little force each time, so it takes a considerable number of taps to drive the nail into the wood. Each time you microdose psilocybin, you are tapping the nail one more time. Eventually, you will get the nail fully into the wood. When you take a heroic dose, it's like using a sledgehammer: driving the nail fully into the wood in a single stroke. Both will get the nail into the wood, but they do so at very different speeds. When taking a heroic dose, one must have a very clear intention with a solid plan and extreme safety measures in place to include a shaman, 'trip sitter,' or under professional doctor care so that you do no harm to yourself or others. In other words, you can bend the nail or split the wood if the force is not applied properly.

This is why I advocate rescheduling psilocybin from Schedule I to Schedule III or IV, to allow further research with much fewer regulatory restrictions. While these medicines have a low potential for addiction, psilocybin in large quantities is too powerful to be left to an unregulated or uneducated market. Let us not repeat the mistakes of our past. In 1970, Richard Nixon 'threw the baby out with the bathwater' and the mental healthcare community has been hampered by this decision for the last 50 years.

The third episode of the docuseries is on MDMA and how it is proving to be an effective treatment for PTSD. My understanding of PTSD, at this time, was very limited. I thought PTSD could only happen from a single horrible event such as a rape, an IED explosion to your vehicle, or a major accident. I knew of several former military people who struggled with PTSD or who had ended their lives because of it. I never believed I had PTSD because I completely disassociated from my early youth, and the traumatic events I could remember did not cause nightmares or other major mental health issues.

As I sat and watched this episode, I found myself drawn into the stories and how effective MDMA was at resolving past traumas. Even though the stories of these traumatized people were completely different than anything I had ever experienced, I felt a strong connection to what they were saying. By the end of watching this episode, there was a part of me that was saying, *"I need me some of that."*

Wait, what!!!

The internal conversation I had with myself after watching this episode is an example of Internal Family Systems: Parts Work. (Promotor Part VS Confused or Denial Part)

Promotor Part said: I need me some of that.

Narrator: A part of me was saying to myself that I could benefit from MDMA because I resonated with their stories.

Confused and Denial part responded: Why do I need this?

Promotor Part states: Because this will help me.

Confused and Denial Part questions: Why would this help us?

Promotor Part states confidently: Don't you see any resemblance to our life and to these stories? If we relate, we probably share some of the qualities of these people who state they have PTSD.

Confused and Denial part: I don't have PTSD! (with denial and anger)

Promoter Part confidently and compassionately responds with: Well, don't you think these stories resonate with you? They sure do with me.

Narrator: The part in denial recognized and related to what the Promotor Part said.

Confused and Denial Part finally asks: Is it possible I do have something like PTSD? Was my estranged wife right all along, but couldn't articulate the difference in what she saw in me and our shared understanding between classical PTSD and what I had?

Over the next several weeks, I finally fully admitted to myself that I had some form of PTSD and that I could possibly benefit from MDMA as a form of medicine to treat PTSD. Honestly, it took me a few months to fully accept my self-diagnosis. In fact, every time I told myself I had PTSD, tears would well up in my eyes, but of course, I wouldn't let them out because 'Real Men Don't Cry.' More on this in Section III.

Over the next few months, I took many opportunities to hold space for and honor these thoughts in private. Over time, I was able to tell myself and accept that I probably had *something like PTSD,* and be able to say this to myself without getting choked up. My limited and somewhat shallow belief of PTSD meant that this diagnosis meant that I was somehow weak and there was something wrong with me if I had this disorder. That having PTSD was my fault, and I should feel shame for being weak. Strong men do not get PTSD, or that is what my father had unknowingly taught me due to his own inability to see himself objectively.

I now know this belief is false and would offer that the D in PTSD should stand for Dysregulation, not Disorder. Because the term "disorder" has a negative connotation, or at least it does for me. What happened to my father and me was not weakness, but we did not have the cognitive tools in our toolbox to properly process and resolve what happened to us *at the time of the trauma*. Therefore, parts of us were stuck in the past, hindering our ability to be good people in the present.

Eventually, I was able to process the emotions associated with this hard truth, and by doing so, I came to acceptance. In other words, I had to let a part of me know that it was OK if I did have PTSD and that I should not feel shame or guilt for this, and that I was OK. My voice of beratement part was not too thrilled with this idea. Telling the Captain, who came into my office crying that he was OK, came easily, but it was much harder for me to tell myself and believe. After all, I had spent a lifetime spewing harsh words to myself.

Once I had fully accepted that I had some form of PTSD and I was able to say these words without any significant emotional response, this revelation became my accepted truth. This meant that I had significant inner work to do.

Admitting to myself that I had something like PTSD was one of the hardest truths I have had to tell myself . . . but it was also one of the most life-changing and best gifts I have ever given myself in return.

I lied to myself and my estranged wife about my PTSD, not because I was a bad person who did not want to face the truth about my trauma. I lied because my understanding of PTSD was deeply flawed. I thought I had escaped from my deeply dysfunctional family because I turned away from drugs and left the chaotic environment so long ago. As a youth and young adult, I sat in my emotions the best my adolescent brain could and processed what I could understand . . . or remember.

I used the knowledge that my college honors psychology courses provided, which gave me the tools to understand my family dysfunction better. Not being able to hit the relief valve that alcohol and marijuana offer as a youth provided me the mental space and *clarity* of mind to be able to process a significant portion of my past through self-realization and self-therapy that my college psychology courses had taught me. In fact, I had somewhat processed many of the traumatic events I remembered by the time I was an adult.

Unfortunately, I was completely ignorant of a deeper level of processing that I didn't even begin to examine due to my go-to coping mechanisms of repressing or dissociating. Like I stated at the beginning of this memoir, my dad only "knew what he knew when he knew it," and I had forgiven him for his shortcomings. It was now my turn to extend this same grace to myself. I can tell you it is so much harder to forgive yourself than it is to forgive others . . . at least it was for me.

Brutal honesty with yourself is what creates the mindset that opens the possibility of transformative healing. It is brutal self-honesty, without judgment, shame, or fear, that opens the door to becoming your highest and best Self.

This I Know!

23

SPIRITUAL AWAKENING

A transformative experience marked by a deeper understanding of oneself, a heightened awareness of the spiritual realm, and often a sense of purpose or connection to something larger than oneself. It can involve a shift in perspective, a renewed faith, or a deeper connection to one's true self.

About the same time that I admitted to myself that I had something like PTSD, I learned about the Stoic philosophy of Amor Fati. *Amor Fati and its principle of acceptance of reality, fate as a teacher, freedom from suffering,* and *cosmic perspective (see page 249 for further details).* It was with this lens that I began to reflect on who I had become and *to find meaning in my life.*

As I reflected on my life while microdosing psilocybin in the hammock, thoughts of my brother and how our shared upbringing had led us down very different paths kept popping into my mind. He had struggled to thrive and be a productive member of society, while, on the surface, I had done well in life. I remembered a conversation I had with my brother during a visit with him at one of the drug rehabilitation facilities he attended. During this visit, he mentioned how he held onto so much shame that he hadn't been able to look at himself in the mirror for quite some time. For some reason, this thought was bouncing in and out of my consciousness over several weeks.

Part of me was extremely saddened by this comment, and another part of me was grateful that I could look myself in the mirror. I began to think about what I would want to tell myself in the mirror to help me get through this storm I was currently in.

I came up with *"Be the best human you can today!!"*

I started to say this affirmation to myself every morning when I woke up and brushed my teeth. The affirmation reminded me that everyone is going through something, especially since COVID, so try to show up in the best way to everyone you meet. At the time, my estranged wife and I's conversations only seemed to reinforce the wounded actions and reactions. This motto or mantra reminded me to just do the best I could, despite the storm clouds that seemed to rain down on me.

With my newfound affirmation or mantra of *"Be the Best Human I can, today,"* and my recent microdosing experiences under my belt, my *perspective* started to open slightly. I began to open my mind to new ideas. This is when I would meet a person who would open my eyes to how deeply my traumatic past had shaped me to become the person I was.

Everyone needs a spiritual teacher, priest, shaman, or, in my case, a twenty-eight-year-old healer/energy worker and yoga instructor who was well-versed in PTSD and trauma. In late May 2023, we met during a commercial property showing where she was considering opening a yoga and wellness space. I was representing the building's owner as their commercial real estate broker. We conducted small talk about what she was looking for and her needs. She mentioned she was attending a multi-day outdoor Electronic Dance Music (EDM) festival in a couple of weeks. She wasn't ready to decide whether to take the space until after the festival.

I knew from my earlier years of attending multi-day outdoor music festivals that psychedelics were part of the culture. Due to my recent revelation that I had something like PTSD, and that MDMA could be an effective tool for unlocking PTSD, this outdoor music festival sparked my interest. We chatted briefly about the festival. She mentioned the festival dates, and they lined up exactly with the dates my house was rented out to Airbnb guests.

After my wife moved out of our house and I was living alone, I started to rent my home at the high end of the local market. I loved my home because it was my safe space, but I felt guilty having an unnecessarily large home for myself. Because of its size and pricing, my home rents for about thirty days per year. I have a two-night minimum, and it mostly rents during the weekends: Friday through Sunday. Once or twice a year, guests will book my home for three or four days straight. Every time I have guests this long, I use it as an opportunity to explore and do something instead of being stuck in my basement apartment for so long. Prior to this commercial showing, I set my intention to go camping over those four days, explore mushrooms more deeply, and possibly do MDMA. I had been busy at work, so I hadn't had time to determine where I was going to go camping.

Because I showed some interest in the music festival, this young lady mentioned that I should attend. Her offer to go to a music festival where they were playing EDM, doing yoga, and offering other holistic healing experiences, for some reason, seemed like the exact thing I needed. Shortly after our meeting, I made the quick decision to go. I let her know my intention, and we chatted briefly through text. She informed me that she was planning to go to the festival alone due to a recent breakup and suggested that we form an alliance and camp together. I assumed she was apprehensive about going with me even as she extended the invite. I recognized that I was much older (25 years older), so I wanted to put her mind at ease that I was not some creepy old man. I texted her this proposal:

"If we do form an alliance, this is my promise to you, I will only treat you with love and respect. You do you . . . and I'll do me. No judgment, no negative energy, no obligation (other than the buddy system and making sure the other has a great safe experience). If this is agreeable, I am in."

She agreed!

I sent this text to her because I wanted to focus on myself and further explore mushrooms and potentially try MDMA. I knew I was going to let some of my 'weird' out and didn't want any distractions from this inner work. My viewing of the 3rd episode of the Netflix series *How to Change Your Mind* also set my intention that MDMA might be effective as a modality for treatment of my "PTSD like" symptoms. Once I committed to going to the music festival, I knew I was going to do some mushrooms and MDMA at it. As we planned for the trip, she mentioned she was into 'extracurriculars' with a mushroom emoji. We quickly realized we were both good humans looking for a fun and safe experience exploring psychedelics to expand our enjoyment of the festival.

Once at the festival, we set up our joint camping site and got through some of the initial awkwardness by chatting a bit about who we were and what made us tick. As the sun was getting low in the sky, we decided to take some mushrooms to relax a bit. I think we were both a little apprehensive, so we pinched off a small section of a stem and took the same amount.

Before we took the mushrooms, she asked me to set my intention for the medicine. I was not expecting this language from her, so I asked her to explain. She mentioned how she takes psychedelics, not to 'check out' but to 'check in' or something to this effect. Her thoughtfulness in being respectful and mindful of what we were about to partake in put my mind at ease. At this point, I was starting to see that she was a good person and that I didn't have to worry about some drug-addicted young mess popping out of nowhere.

We both set our intentions and took a very low recreational dose of mushrooms. Enough to know you felt different, but not enough to cause one to trip. At most, it was about .5 grams each. After a while, the medicine was starting to take effect and relax both of us a bit, and she opened up about her life.

As she described her life, we quickly realized we had very similar experiences but different timelines because I was 25 years older than her. We both did gymnastics at a young age; we both were college cheerleaders for the college or university we attended. We both came from VERY dysfunctional families! As she opened up about her life, she mentioned that she had *Complex PTSD (CPTSD).* I was very familiar with PTSD due to my war experiences, but I had never heard of CPTSD. She explained that CPTSD was much different and that it manifested from repeated trauma from her extended family, and for her, at a very early age.

During the festival, we both found ourselves in a very safe mental space. She opened up a lot about her past traumas, and I shared a few things as well. She stated that she had blocked out much of her early childhood and didn't remember anything about her early childhood abuse. She told me the story about how she had recovered her memories only about five years prior and how these early traumatic experiences manifested as CPTSD for her. She told me how disruptive it was to get her early childhood memories back and her healing journey in the subsequent five years. Since recovering her childhood memories, she had spent significant time researching CPTSD and the modalities, tools, and techniques to treat trauma in her journey toward healing. She introduced me to Richard Schwartz's Internal Family Systems approach to trauma, and how yoga, music, Eye Movement Desensitization and Reprocessing (EMDR), and other tools and techniques were useful tools for her in dealing with trauma. Her knowledge of the subject was very impressive. I was fascinated by the things she was describing, which helped her to reunite with various parts of herself, thus heal from and move past. It is a great story, but hers to tell.

As they say, "When the student is ready, the teacher will appear."

I believe the universe/god (God) put us together for a reason, and our meeting was cosmic synchronicity. Everyone needs a teacher or elder, and we were both able to hold this space for each other. In my case, I needed a much more spiritually connected person who was much further down the path of healing from CPTSD to educate me about what I was about to discover about my own past. She needed someone with a similar dysfunctional family, but much older, who could relate to and hold a safe space to help her process as well. Our friendship blossomed and grew out of mutual respect and compassion for each other's experiences growing up.

24

TAROT READING

Tarot is a deck of seventy-eight cards organized into categories designed to provide insight into a person's past, present, or future.

At the outdoor music festival (June 8-11, 2023), my camping partner introduced me to tarot cards. I had never done a tarot reading before and wasn't particularly interested in what they had to offer, but I listened. Before this experience, I knew very little about tarot and felt that tarot cards were just a random-guessing tool that people used to try to find meaning in their lives, and that the cards would randomly match something you could find meaning in. In other words, we humans try to find meaning in randomness that just isn't there.

She did a tarot reading on me three times at the festival. In every reading, the Five of Cups card came up. This card is generally known as "The Grief" card (see above). On the first reading, I didn't know what this card meant. She explained to me that the Grief card may indicate that I have unresolved grief in my life and that I may have something stuck in the past that I can't let go of, or words to this effect. Since this was all new to me, I passed it off as a random card. Of course, I knew grief. Doesn't everyone know grief by the time they are as old as I am?

On the second night of the festival, she pulls out the tarot deck once again and does a slightly different reading with a different layout of cards. Again, the Five of Cups was played, and she reminded me of what this card could mean depending on the context in which it came up in the reading.

On the third day of the festival, we were sitting in the shade on the hill just above the performance stages in the early afternoon, and she pulled out the tarot deck for our third and final reading. We had done a low-dose mixture of mushrooms and MDMA each of the two previous nights, but we had not consumed any drugs this day, other than a high CBD (10 mg) and low THC (1 mg) edible for the soreness that occurs after multiple days of dancing and yoga. During this reading, the Grief card was laid for the third time in a row. For some reason, the magnitude of what the Grief card represented hit me and hit me hard!

Immediately, I wondered, *what are the odds of getting the Grief card three times in a row?* Even the skeptical side of my brain recognized the pattern that was emerging and couldn't be denied. I had an internal dialogue. I said to myself, *"Wow, what the fuck just happened?"*

By this point at the festival, I had spent the last two nights processing some of my unresolved grief. On the first night, as I took the MDMA, I thought of my dead dog and sent him my love and said goodbye. The reason I set that intention was my dog kept popping up into my mind while I was microdosing mushrooms the summer prior. When he first began popping back into my mind the previous summer, I couldn't even say his name. It took me many weeks to be able to say his name, *RAMBO,* to myself. That night, it felt really good to reflect on him and to love my dog one last time as I was under the effects of the medicine.

While under the effects of the medicine, I realized that I never properly or fully mourned his death. I had repressed or stuffed these emotions aside due to being so focused on how my dad would respond if he found out what actually happened that night. I was so focused on burying my dog and the cover-up that I never properly or fully processed this event.

On the following night, while I was under the effects of MDMA, I mourned and grieved all of those who had died and been killed in Iraq . . . including my enemies. I came to a compassionate understanding that we were all doing the best we could, based on the information we had at the time. Unfortunately, war is a nasty business that causes the taking of lives on all sides.

During this reflection, I focused on the human emotions that go along with killing or death, not only my own emotions but the emotions of those around me. I kept saying to myself, *"Well, that was fucked up."*

As I said these things to myself, I seemed to come to a sense of understanding or acceptance that what I was a part of was never right and never will be right, but that it is okay and that I am okay—now! MDMA provided me the *compassion* to examine my past and the *clarity* to accept in ways I couldn't seem to do previously.

Because I had spent the last two nights letting go of grief, this card hit me *HARD*. In that moment, I realized that I had been holding onto the grief of these events and others for way too long and that I had been stuck in grief since my wife and I separated.

On that card, I see myself as the man in the black coat, head down. The pain and attitude of my suffering during the last several years were staring me in the face, and I could not deny it. I think my spiritual teacher and camping buddy was taken aback as well.

She looked at me, with a soft kindness in her eyes, and said in a compassionate tone, “You’ve seen a lot of grief, haven’t you?”

By this point, I had shared a little about my military background and some of my childhood. I couldn’t hide it anymore. I said, “YES!”

As I admitted this out loud, tears began to roll down my face for the first time in a very long time. Her amazing openness to her own early childhood trauma, coupled with her compassionate and kind spirit, and the lasting effects of MDMA, created a safe space for me to finally be able to cry in front of someone. I somehow sensed that this card was telling me that it was time to let go of my grief for good, as it was obvious that grief was no longer serving me.

This card represented how a part of me had felt for so long as I looked upon the man in the black coat, facing down.

Grief had been me . . . or at least a part of me for quite some time.

As I stared at the sullen man on the tarot card who looked so deflated, I heard a small childlike voice in my head say, *“This is not me!”*

I am confused as to where this tiny voice comes from. I start to have an internal conversation with this childlike voice in my head.

I ask this voice, *“What do you mean, ‘this is not me?’”*

As I ask the question, I am telling myself, *“This sullen man absolutely has been me . . . and for way too long, if I am being completely honest.”*

The little voice in my head says, “*That MAN is not me,*” as it directs my attention to the right of the defeated man.

Next to the man, I see two big, inquisitive, and innocent bright eyes staring up at the sullen man, whom I see as me. This little voice says, *“THIS IS ME!”*

Once I lock onto the big eyes that sit at the feet just right of the grieving man, the little voice asks me, "*Is it safe to come out?*"

I ask this little voice in a thoroughly confused tone, "*What do you mean, 'is it safe to come out?' YES, of course, it is safe to come out.*"

As I process this internal conversation, I am baffled about where the little voice comes from. I chuckle to myself as tears roll down my cheeks.

I tell my camping buddy, "I see myself in both. I have been stuck in grief, but I am ready to come out of grief and look at the world again with bright, inquisitive eyes."

The big eyes I saw were actually the bridge to the lower right of the deflated man, but in my mind at the time, they represented a much earlier part of me asking whether it was safe to come out of hiding. It will take me five months and another round of MDMA and psilocybin to fully understand where this conversation manifested from and to get my early childhood memories back.

What I learned five months later was that this little voice was the three-year-old *'Exiled'* part of me (IFS parts work) that had been imprisoned and locked away in a back room of my basement of lost memories. This exiled part of me was showing itself for the first time in 50 years. This part of me was finally coming out of hiding and looking out into the world for the first time in five decades, with the innocence of a three-year-old.

In my internal conversation with myself, I was telling different versions of myself that it was safe for the three-year-old version of me to come out of hiding, and it was safe for the adult version of me to come out of grief.

This I Know!

25

RECOVERED MEMORIES & INTERNAL FAMILY SYSTEMS (IFS) PARTS WORK

You can't understand what you can't recall. IFS provides a valuable framework for exploring the depths of our being, reconnecting with our inner child, and empowering us to live more authentic, fulfilling lives.

Upon returning from the festival, I felt really amazing. I felt as though a giant weight had been lifted off me. I had said a loving goodbye to my dog Rambo. I had mourned the loss of life I had seen and the apparent dissolving of my marriage. The world no longer felt crushing or overwhelming. I had somehow gained some control of my life, and I had the energy to face each day with newfound vigor. If I am being honest, I felt several years younger.

What I have recently learned is that psilocybin can increase mitochondria production and efficiency in your cells. Increased mitochondria, which are the energy-producing factories of the cell, provided this boost in energy. I utilized this newfound energy to begin to practice yoga regularly and to treat myself better by eating properly. My life energy was so much better, and I didn't want it to go away, so I began to take much better care of myself. All of this helped me to integrate and thus transform out of some of the grief and despair I had been in . . . and to lose about fifteen pounds along the way.

Fast forward four months, and to my fifty-fourth birthday on October 28th, 2023. I decided that I did not want to celebrate my birthday with anyone, but to learn more about myself. I was still blown away by how much better I felt after the festival, but I knew there was more to learn and discover about myself. I wanted to do a deep cognitive dive because I still felt I was missing something and still had times where the old me was trying to creep back in. So, I decided to do MDMA and psilocybin in combination again for the first time since the festival.

As part of my risk-mitigation strategy for my psilocybin/MDMA journey, I set the boundary not to leave my house for any reason. I locked my car keys in a safe, put notes on each exterior door that stated *DO NOT LEAVE THE FOUR CORNERS OF THE PROPERTY.* In fact, I relegated myself to my basement apartment for the journey. I decided I would once again take a low recreational dose of mushrooms, somewhere near 0.5 grams, so I could settle into my intention with a *calm* mind as we had done at the festival.

At the festival, we always started with psilocybin and allowed 1-2 hours before consuming the MDMA. For me, psilocybin at low doses helps me be more present and quiets the distractions in my mind. I feel I can be more present or intentional. I waited just over an hour after consuming the mushrooms to allow the effects to kick in. Once I felt fully relaxed and calm in my mind, I asked myself, *"What do I want to learn about myself?"* For reasons I cannot explain, I wanted to go back to my early childhood. Perhaps it was because of what my camping partner and spiritual teacher had shared with me about recovering her early childhood memories. I didn't remember any of my early childhood, but knew that by the time I entered school, I was afraid of my father, but did not remember any trauma before getting my nose broken in the fifth grade.

As I took the MDMA, I said my intention out loud: "Why did *I have a visceral fear and hatred for my father by the time I entered kindergarten?"* As I was waiting for the MDMA to kick in, I turned on my stereo and began to clean and organize my basement as I listened to music. Once the medicine was flowing through me, I started to stretch and dance while trying to remember my early childhood involving my father. I reflected on what I could remember of my youth.

As early as I can remember, it was kindergarten. I remembered the time I was pulling weeds at one of my dad's rental properties with a broken collarbone. I had broken my collarbone playing baseball in the neighbor's yard a few days earlier. I complained to my father that I couldn't pull weeds because it hurt. He informed me that I still had one good arm, so I was to use it. While it made me a little angry because I didn't get out of pulling weeds, it wasn't that big of a deal. I came across similar memories, yet nothing that evoked any strong or visceral feelings. I also couldn't seem to penetrate any earlier memory than the broken collarbone. At this point, I couldn't remember being spanked with anger at ages much later than this. I had completely blocked these events and any memory of my bedwetting and subsequent beatings due to my trauma response of disassociation. Eventually, I got tired and went to bed. I woke up the next day and thought . . . well, that didn't work. I wondered what I had done wrong that I did not get the answers I had been seeking.

Fast forward to the following Thursday and five days after I took the MDMA. I didn't have a busy work schedule and was feeling rather somber and introspective. Perhaps it was the serotonin letdown that can happen after taking MDMA. So, I decided to be good to myself and just let the day happen (integration). I decided to get a bento box from my favorite local sushi restaurant.

As I was finishing my last bite of sashimi, I received a memory so clear that I felt as though I was experiencing it in the present. The memory of being woken up by my screaming father, of being yanked out of bed, and being thrown into the cabinets, on the wall beside my bed—all came back to me in full color. This memory came back to me with all the sights, sounds, pains, and emotions I had at the moment it was preserved in me.

The memory was so vivid and strong that tears began to roll down both cheeks as I was feeling the stabbing pain of the cabinet handle strike my back, and sensing the adrenaline and panic quickly rise in the three-year-old version of myself as he bounced off the cabinets. My body was being flooded with these hormones, and my breathing became rapid as this memory was being revealed to me. I could hear the exact words my father was saying as he was striking me with the belt across most of my body.

This memory, as you can imagine, hit me like a freight train.

I began to cry for my earlier self. I cried with *compassion* and love for what my earlier self had experienced so long ago. In fact, I had to go to the bathroom to compose myself and create a safe space so I could feel comfortable expressing my tears.

As I stood in the bathroom, I kept telling my three-year-old self, "*It wasn't your fault.*"

On the third or fourth iteration, I instinctively gave my three-year-old self a giant hug of unconditional love, feeling so bad for that kid and somehow knowing that was what he needed.

As I did this, my three-year-old self—who was trapped in the past, frozen like an insect in amber— broke free and hugged me back!

As I felt him embrace me back, I felt something radiate within me that I hadn't felt before. I felt the *unconditional love* that I gave my three-year-old self start to flow into and through adult me.

To truly feel *unconditional love* for the first time is quite a profound experience that is impossible to adequately describe. This love felt like *calmness*, a very warm, peaceful, contented radiance that spread through my body. Similar to how the warm sun feels on your face on a cold day, only I could feel this warmth not only on the surface, but also radiating through my entire body and even into my bones.

This was a mind-blowingly beautiful moment that fills my heart with happiness and gratitude every time I think about it. In this moment, I finally and truly felt what had escaped me for most of my life and what prevented me from being calm or peaceful. I felt love for myself!

It was so much easier for me to love the three-year-old version of myself than it was to love the adult me. Who doesn't love a three-year-old with big, inquisitive, innocent eyes? This is how I began to love myself for the first time in over fifty years. This is how I began to reintegrate an abandoned part of myself and merge the lost three-year-old part of me back with my soul or adult me.

Every time I provided unconditional love to the three-year-old version of myself, the unconditional love I gave him came pouring back into and through my adult self. By loving that little child completely and unconditionally, I, in turn, loved myself.

Crazy huh??

Over the next couple of months, as I was shown this memory again and a multitude of other times I was beaten with rage by my father, I would radically accept whatever was being shown to me, and tell my much younger versions of myself, *"It wasn't your fault!"*

With the passing of each memory, I noticed his feelings of panic, confusion, and anger toward himself, which seemed to soften with every recollection.

As his panic and fear softened, I noticed my adult mind became clearer. My voice of beratement volume was being turned down and eventually . . . got turned off. As this was happening, my mind was becoming clearer, and my energy was becoming *calmer*. I began to realize that the voice in my head that had berated me for any of my mistakes for the last fifty years was not me. I came to realize that the internal voice of beratement were the words of my father that I had somehow embodied as if they were my own!! I began to realize that I was not the 'voice of beratement' but that I was *the divinity of the silence beneath it.* (More on this later.)

By loving myself and resolving the traumatic event so very long ago, I was able to quiet this internal voice of beratement.

At first, I did not understand the connection between my memories and my internal voice of beratement. What I have learned since is that I locked in my dad's harsh and hurtful words with these traumatic memories, and I have been using these harsh words against myself for most of my life. I am not even sure those words were my father's, as I believe he was just recycling his father's words, which were imprinted on him.

These harmful and hateful words were screamed from one generation to the next with anger and rage that somehow became my responsibility to carry forward. These harsh and hateful words have been part of me for so long that I didn't even recognize they were there or understand where or how they manifested within me. I had processed the trauma, and subsequently, I released the grip of self-beratement from myself.

Life changing!!

As I was integrating this newfound information and exiled part of me, I realized that, even though I was telling myself to *"Be the best human I can today,"* I couldn't be a good human to others when I wasn't being a very good human to myself first. So shortly after this revelation, I changed my morning affirmation to *"Be the best human you can be to yourself and others!"* This epiphany and modified affirmation *greatly accelerated my transformation journey.*

I also began to piece together that the small, childlike voice I first heard during the last tarot reading at the music festival over four months prior was the same exiled part of me asking whether it was safe to come out.

I journaled: *Today is November 12th, 2023, and I now realize that the person looking out and asking if it was safe to come out at the festival was the three-year-old version of myself that had been locked up inside me and afraid to come out for 50 years.*

> Holy fuck!!
>
> How is it possible that a part of me was locked away and imprisoned in my subconscious?
>
> How is it that my dad's hurtful and hateful words became my own . . . to myself? . . . and how was I completely oblivious to all of it?

I consider myself to be pretty smart or aware, but WOW, I was walking around in complete denial or complete ignorance or whatever you want to call it.

While I do not fully understand the science of how MDMA works for trauma, I am thoroughly convinced that it was the MDMA that allowed my three-year-old 'exiled part' of me to feel safe enough to come out of hiding. Perhaps it was the rush of serotonin, dopamine, and norepinephrine that is released as part of an MDMA experience, which put my mind and body into a state of safety and broke free this exiled part.

By getting the memories back, I was able to recall and remember the traumatic events that I had held as unresolved trauma for way too long. This memory was like the bottom log in a log dam; once it was removed, the floodgates opened to other memories, allowing me to understand not only who I had become . . . but why! They were like puzzle pieces that fell into place, giving me clarity to see myself objectively and the background to understand why I behaved in certain ways.

Now that I have enough life experiences and the mental framework regarding trauma, I am able to see these memories through a new *perspective.* With this new perspective, I was able to provide love, comfort, and compassion for the earlier versions of myself that didn't get the love or emotional support they needed, nor did my younger self have the cognitive tools to fully understand, address, or process. How could he—he was only three, five, ten, thirteen!

I feel so blessed and grateful to finally love myself and reunite with the lost parts of myself! I never knew what I was missing until I felt it. I wish my father could have felt this for himself. If he had felt the love I was now feeling, he never could have pulled the trigger that ended his life. My dad never loved himself, and I am pretty sure his father never loved himself either. Self-beratement/hatred was the family secret; we Holt men carried through the generations. With this newfound love for myself, I am now able to find the peace, happiness, and contentment that had escaped me for my entire life.

After getting my memories back, I scheduled a rare session with my therapist. I told her about the music festival and the tarot reading, about utilizing psilocybin and MDMA, and about how I connected to my three-year-old self. I told her everything. As I walked out of the building where her office was located, music was playing from a neighboring restaurant's patio. I heard the song "Iris" from the Goo Goo Dolls, and the first words I heard were:

And I don't want the world to see me
'Cause I don't think that they'd understand
When everything's made to be broken
I just want you to know who I am

For some strange reason, I immediately knew this was a sign from the universe (Clair cognizance), and these lyrics were my three-year-old self telling adult me how he felt and why he had hidden for 50 years. Having a father who beat him and broke his nose, plus having an older brother who routinely beat him as well, and eventually stabbed him, too. These early childhood experiences caused him and other parts of me to hide because the world felt unsafe to them. They lacked the cognitive and emotional support they needed at the time these events occurred, which led them all to feel unworthy of love. By sharing the painful memories with adult me and my ability to provide the comfort and care these parts needed so long ago, they could heal and no longer had to be imprisoned unjustly.

In this moment of realization, I knew why I had always felt alone and different, as though no one would ever understand me. Because I can now see the imprinting that this idea instilled inside of me as a very young child, as part of my response to trauma.

Shortly afterward, as my journaling began to take on a form with stories and lessons learned, I felt there might be a story worth telling others so that they could learn from my shortcomings and my transformation or healing journey.

As part of my 'parts' work, I asked the three-year-old part of me, *"Do you trust me to tell your story?"*

He told me he did, as long as I told his story in a loving way, which the world would hopefully understand. This memoir, in part, is a loving tribute to my three-year-old self. Additionally, this memoir is also a loving tribute to my mother and father, who died from opposite ends of the suicide spectrum, for their inability to process their emotions, trauma, and pain.

Song from Emmitt Sisters: *ho'oponopono*

I'm sorry,
I forgive you,
Thank you,
I love you.

. . .

Thank you for the breaking
Thank you for the pain
For without you in my life
I may not be finding myself again

. . .

Love, it doesn't go away
It lives right below the fear and the pain.

Once you process the fear and pain, it opens up the opportunity for Love to rise up and show itself.

This I Know!

26

DEEPER DIVE

Inner cognitive work is the process of getting to know yourself through introspection. Letting go of harmful attachments, habits, people, and thoughts is powerful.

In Early December 2023, I thought to myself, "*If I had hidden away my three-year-old self and not processed any of my early trauma, what else have I hidden*?"

This caused me to feel a need to take a deeper dive into psychedelic medicine. I knew that going any deeper into the medicine and myself was going to require the help of professionals; otherwise, I would be at risk for a bad or potentially harmful experience. So, I reached out through various channels to see what might be available in the U.S.

I found a few people or places that offer a guided heroic journey utilizing psilocybin mushrooms. Finding any reputable location with a long track record of success in this guided inner work was very difficult, if not impossible, to find . . . at least for me. The places I could find couldn't fully or adequately describe the process or experience due to the secrecy that surrounds this work, as it is an illegal Schedule I drug that has no accepted medical use. This is one of the many reasons I believe that legalization through rescheduling to Schedule III, at a minimum, should be seriously considered. This lack of information, regulation, or reviews of past participants did not give me the confidence I needed to entrust my brain to them.

During this outreach, I fell down a YouTube rabbit hole. I researched trauma, PTSD, and Complex PTSD, which is where I found Dr. Gabor Mate, Dr. Bessel van der Kolk, and I did more research on Dr. Richard Schwartz and his Internal Family Systems. These resources are free, so anyone with a computer or a smartphone can access their wisdom. So much of what I have pieced together regarding my life is due to something these and other trauma-informed experts said in an interview, during a podcast, or in a book of theirs that I read.

I used their trauma-informed mental health framework to examine my life and the lives of those around me. It was their trauma-informed *perspectives* that opened my mind to see things differently and to piece together not only who I had become . . . but why. If you go to www.aboynamedpooh.com/help, you will find many videos and links to helpful information on many of the topics I cover, organized around different solutions.

Additionally, as I started to research trauma and sacred plant medicine, I learned about ayahuasca. Ayahuasca is an entheogen or spiritual medicine that can have profound and lasting effects for those who have PTSD, drug addiction, as well as other mental disturbances or physical ailments. As someone who had borne witness to or been a part of a multitude of traumatic events, this medicine seemed very powerful . . . yet appropriate. I found a couple of places that were doing ayahuasca ceremonies in the U.S., but not much information could be gathered due to it being illegal in the U.S. The lack of regulation and the limited information I could gather led me to expand my search outside the U.S., since I wanted to go to a place where I could feel very safe and where those administering these powerful medicines had extensive experience.

I had recently fallen in love with Costa Rica and had been there a couple of times over the last five years, so I googled "Ayahuasca Costa Rica." In this search, I found a seven-day retreat center that was medically licensed and used ayahuasca as its medicine. Their website discussed the various aspects of their program, which had attracted over 15,000 people. Everything that I had found useful in my healing journey thus far was a part of the program at this retreat center. It felt as though they had dialed in the experience and knew what they were doing. Modalities such as yoga, breathwork, somatic massages, and organic, mostly plant-based meals were all part of this all-inclusive program. I decided to reach out to them and learn more.

I spoke to an amazing lady on the phone. I shared my recent childhood PTSD discovery and that I now suspected that my severe hand tremors were at least partially from my childhood trauma and not necessarily a genetically inherited disorder. She was familiar with what I was beginning to understand. She articulately explained the science behind my belief. She discussed how all mammals shake after a traumatic experience, including humans, as a natural and instinctual way to discharge built-up survival energy and restore balance to their nervous system.

She used the example of a gazelle being chased by a lion. When a lion chases a gazelle, and it escapes, once it reaches a safe space, it will begin to shake violently. This is how the gazelle releases the excess, fear-driven energy and brings the nervous system back into balance.

She went on to discuss that if we do not allow ourselves to shake, we can create a blockage in our amygdala that can lock in this shaking. Her calm and caring attitude, mixed with her in-depth knowledge of how trauma can be stored in the body, immediately put my mind at ease. For someone who struggled to trust people, I was quickly in a place of trust, and I knew this was the place for me.

So, in late December 2023, I reached out to my estranged wife to ask her permission to attend this expensive retreat since we were still financially tied together. Somewhat to my surprise, she immediately supported my desire, so I booked a one-week stay and planned to attend at the end of February 2024.

Those who have experienced ayahuasca or Mother Aya, as we like to call her, say the medicine (ayahuasca) starts to work as soon as you are called to it. Once I booked my trip, I began journaling daily. As I was doing this, significant emotional and physical manifestations were occurring during my journaling sessions, which caused my shaking to become worse.

27

THE POWER OF JOURNALING

Trauma journaling is a therapeutic practice that can provide emotional release, improved self-awareness, gain perspective and coping mechanisms, and promote healing.

As someone who had disassociated, repressed, and locked away so many unresolved memories and experiences, I began to piece together how I got to where I was through journaling. With my mind blown by how an exiled part of me could have such a profound impact on my life, I journaled to piece together other memories and start putting my life back together. Journaling provided me with a safe place to express my thoughts, feelings, and anger, where no one else would get hurt, and where I could begin to connect the dots in my life. This process opened the window to explore lost or unknown aspects of my life. Journaling provided meaning to my life, as the Stoic philosophy of Amor Fati pointed me toward.

What I didn't understand when I began this process was how healing it would be. Trauma journaling provided me the space to explore memories and begin to ask questions about them, and examine them through the lens of trauma. With a framework in place around the memories, I was able to attach meaning or resolution to them.

One of the weirdest physical manifestations that occurred was an intense pain I felt in my left forearm. This pain accompanied getting the memory back of me being tossed out of bed by my left wrist. Right after getting this memory back, an intense pain in my left forearm appeared, and the pain grew over several days.

My forearm, right below the elbow, where the connection point of my tendon meets the bone, became extremely inflamed and painful to the touch after getting the memory back. It felt like a deep bone bruise or a bone cancer. Over the next few weeks, it didn't seem to want to go away. I started to have thoughts that I should consider going to the doctor for treatment, as it lasted for almost a month, with significant pain. In fact, even as I write this paragraph over a year later, I can find the point on my bone where it still hurts if I press on it. While I do not understand how or why the body keeps the score, I am convinced that it does after experiencing this.

By examining memories with a new *perspective*, I was able to release so much stored trauma and pain, which in turn energized me and provided me the motivation that had escaped me for the last several years. Before my transformative journey, I had suffered from chronic inflammation and pain for years that seemed to start or greatly accelerate after returning from war the first time. I can honestly say from the time just prior to taking MDMA and psilocybin together until just after the time I did ayahuasca, I felt at least ten years younger. I felt so much more energized than before I began my healing journey . . . and I still do!

On Sunday, November 12th, 2023—just over a week after recovering my three-year-old memories—I sent this text to my sister: (actual text)

"Hi (sister), I hope you are doing well. I have been down a rabbit hole and working on getting myself healthy (physically and cognitively). I wanted to share my most recent revelation and see if it meshes with your memories.

My Complex PTSD began between 3 and 6 years old. It was due to my extended bedwetting. I wet the bed due to the stress I saw what was happening to my older siblings.

My father felt that I was a lazy child who didn't have the discipline to get out of bed to use the bathroom. He felt his best method to resolve this shortcoming was through beating this child with the belt and checking his bed every morning until the bed wetting stopped. As we used to joke in the Marine Corps, "The beatings will continue until morale improves."

Ironic huh?? The difference was that in the Marine Corps, this was a joke we told to each other to provide perspective, as in . . . it could actually be worse. Only in my case, I was somewhere between 3 and 6 years old (I believe) . . . and I didn't have the cognitive growth to fully rationalize. How could I? I was only 6."

About 10 minutes after sending this text, I received a call from my sister. I answer the phone and can tell she is sobbing!

The first words out of her mouth were, "I always hated dad for this."

Hearing this gave me a huge smile and great comfort, knowing that I got it right (mostly) and that the memory I received was real. I let her know that I held no ill will against our father and that he was doing the best he could at the time, but just didn't know better. In other words, I was consoling her and trying to help her heal from the pain of her witnessing my beatings (vicarious trauma) so many years ago.

She also provided insight that I didn't have. She said that I wasn't wetting the bed because of their abuse, although I am sure it contributed to it, but because I had severe asthma as a child. At this point, I did not know how young I was when I was yanked out of my bed and beaten; I only knew it happened before kindergarten. So, over the next few days, I learned that children enter kindergarten at age five, so I narrowed the timing to between three and five.

I sat with my feelings, thoughts, and newfound memories, and asked myself, "How young was I when this happened?" as I had learned from a YouTube video on Internal Family Systems parts work. The number three kept popping into my head.

I was like, "*Are you sure? Not four or five?*"

The age three kept coming back to me, so this is where and how I landed on three years old.

For me, confirmation became liberation. Liberation created the *clarity* I had been seeking in my introspective journey. It felt so . . . so fucking good . . . to finally truly understand not only who I had become . . . but why!

Journaling is not so important that you get it right from the start, but it provides you with the start and the direction to keep going inward. Journaling may not be appropriate to share with others unless the person you share with can hold a safe space for you and your thoughts without taking offense, judgment, or adopting your negative or angry energy. This is what a good therapist does. I shared my revelation with my sister because she could corroborate my memories and offer a different perspective. I knew my sister would know the answer, after all, she was almost 6 years older. I knew that she could help me better understand what I had just unblocked and was trying to make sense of.

Journaling should be your safe space to let your thoughts and feelings pour onto the page. You may find that some of those thoughts and feelings do not represent your most authentic self. You may see that some of these words are negative, or hateful, or would be harmful if you said them to others. The beauty of journaling is that you can release those negative emotions that are stored inside of you without inflicting collateral damage on others around you, thus continuing the trauma cycle humanity is currently stuck in.

Journaling also allows you to reflect on these negative feelings when you are in a different mindset or a better headspace. You may not recognize the words that you wrote, which were so meaningful at the time; they may not represent who you are or how you feel when you are in a much calmer, less triggered emotional state.

You may think, "*What the hell was I thinking or feeling at that time?*"

You may start to see patterns.

You may even see how your language changes when you are triggered or angry.

It is quite possible that your ability to use large words or complex sentence structure is lacking. This could be you telling yourself that an exiled (younger) part is controlling you, or you were not able to think clearly due to your emotional state, as my words have done for me.

You must have *compassion* for all the words you write. Have *compassion* for the triggered part of you who spewed those awful, hateful words. Provide yourself with grace and hold gratitude that you only put those words on paper and did not direct the pain and anger toward anyone else. Journaling not only helps you heal but can prevent you from passing on the negative effects that your unresolved negative experiences or traumas have caused you, as was the case when the senior Marine officer had a violent emotional outburst at the doctor after the doctor saved the enemy combatant's life.

For me, when journaling some of my most painful memories, I would sometimes shake so bad that I had to stop typing because I was physically unable to hit the right key on my laptop. This was my clue to stop and give myself *compassion*. During this process, I let myself shake uncontrollably, and when tears started to well up in my eyes, I let them pour down my face.

Other times, I would start sweating profusely under my arms while being chilled to the bone. In fact, I had to stop many times and take a steaming hot shower to regulate my internal temperature to feel warm again. Releasing trauma through journaling can be that powerful and overwhelming. It was for me!

While I did not know how or why I had these visceral physical reactions to memories that occurred so long ago, I did know that I had to allow them to manifest, honor them, and let them out if they were to be released for good. Dr. Bessel van der Kolk taught me this, and I am extremely grateful for his teachings. Removing stored trauma is how one moves on and heals. Journaling became cathartic; it became my safe place to release my emotions and honor them, no matter how they presented themselves.

In the two and a half months of journaling while I was awaiting my trip to Costa Rica, I allowed myself to cry many more times than I had in the previous thirty-plus years. With those tears came relief and resolve. Additionally, about a year later, I found a therapist who was trained in Eye Movement Desensitization and Reprocessing (EMDR). She had me review many of my most traumatic events while undergoing the EMDR protocol with hand buzzers. My body reacted similarly to how it reacted during my initial trauma journaling. Both created visceral somatic reactions and shaking, thus they seem to work in similar ways to help resolve stored trauma. I highly recommend both!!

As I reflect on the importance of journaling to me, I recall the letter I briefly mentioned earlier in this memoir. I wrote this letter to myself when I was in college. This letter contained all of the things I was not going to do to my own children because of the pain and suffering my father's actions or inactions had caused my siblings and me.

This letter, while poorly constructed, thoughtfully outlined the pains of growing up with an abusive father. When I found the letter many years later, I remember thinking how poorly the letter was written.

"I was in college when I wrote this?" I thought. *"It looks like a child wrote it."*

I also remember that I was angry toward my father when I wrote it. It was written when I was emotionally triggered, so my use of long sentences or proper grammar was very much lacking.

Once I got past the poorly constructed sentences and paragraphs and began to understand the message, it became apparent to me that it was spot-on and powerful! It was also very liberating and validating to read those words fifteen-ish years later and know that I had mostly kept my promises to myself. It felt really good to know that I mostly did not put the same stresses and strains on my children that I was passionate enough to commit to while in college.

In the few times that I did not keep to my word, I was in a triggered emotional state due to unresolved trauma, which caused me to pass on my generational trauma and to spank my own child with anger for wetting the bed. I had repressed my memories so deeply that I didn't even know they were there. Had I processed my early childhood memories instead of repressing and disassociating from them, I never would have gotten so emotionally triggered and spanked my son with anger for wetting the bed. Instead, I would have hugged him and let him know that it was okay, that he was okay, and that mistakes happen to all of us, and that I used to wet the bed. I didn't do this because I didn't remember.

You can't resolve what you can't remember or can't control.

This I Know!

28

THE POWER OF THE PURGE

Trauma is what is stored in your body, and purgative medicines like ayahuasca help to remove the trauma from the body so these negative past events and their emotional dysregulations do not affect your present.

After trauma journaling the last couple of months, I attended the ayahuasca retreat's seven-day program in Costa Rica in Feb 2024. As part of the program, I was in class for several hours each day. During this classwork, they taught us about ayahuasca and how it works. I learned that ayahuasca is a purgative medicine that facilitates the release of negative thoughts, feelings, and patterns that no longer serve you. In other words, purging is how these self-limiting beliefs, harmful behaviors, and trauma get released from the body. After all, it is the body that keeps the score.

At the resort medical-spa, they would constantly remind us that *what is coming . . . is going* and is part of the process of release. While the journey may not be enjoyable at the time, the medicine brings up and out emotions, repressed or painful experiences, and memories, so just breathe, observe, and let the process happen. Try not to fight or hold onto the distress, as one must purge the feelings and emotions that are stored with these traumatic memories to move past them properly.

Purging can take many forms: laughing hysterically, crying uncontrollably, yawning incessantly, or vomiting or diarrhea. Don't stress about these aspects! You have enough control to engage in these activities with dignity.

I was blessed with a powerful purge on my first night under the medicine. Yes, you heard me. I was blessed to purge—and purge violently. During the ceremony, most people in the room consume 1-2 cups of ayahuasca to go under the medicine and be fully under its effect. I had to take five cups before the medicine would begin to affect me. Here is what I experienced during my first journey:

As I begin my first ceremony, I line up inside the ceremonial maloca with fifty others to receive the medicine. As I take my first cup of ayahuasca, I state my intention out loud: "Show me who I have become." I walk back to my twin mattress and lie on it with a clean bottom sheet, blanket, pillow, my private bucket, and a roll of toilet paper. A few minutes later, everyone in the room has finished taking the medicine, and we all lay down in silence for the next hour to give the first cup of the medicine time to be absorbed. About halfway through the hour of our noble silence, I hear others begin to cry, laugh, or vomit. I giggle to myself as I begin to realize that this is going to be one weird night. As I lie on my mattress, I am thinking that I will find myself in a similar situation soon, but for the time being, I am completely awake and sober.

After an hour of lying down without any noticeable effects, the head shaman calls for the second cup for those who are not fully under its effects. I get up, stand in line, receive my medicine, and say again, "Show me who I have become." I return to my mattress and lie in stillness while I await the medicine's effects. The person lying next to me starts waving his arms above him in a robotic motion that doesn't seem natural. I am initially intrigued by what he is doing. It is as if his arms are scanning devices and tools. I decide I need to stop paying attention to him and put on the eye mask I was given so I can focus on myself and what is to be my journey. As I lay there stone sober listening to others around me moan, puke, laugh, or cry for another thirty minutes, I realize that the first two cups of ayahuasca are doing nothing to alter my consciousness.

I am completely sober as I listen to the evening unfold. For some reason, I feel nothing from the medicine even though it is very obvious that most around me are now fully under its effects.

When it is time to take a third cup if needed, I proceed to the front where the shaman and other lightworkers are sitting. I ask for a third cup of the medicine. The shaman asks me if I have yawned, cried, laughed, or used the bathroom before handing me another cup of the medicine. She does this to gauge whether she should give me another cup and how much medicine to put in it.

I take my third cup and return to my mattress on the floor. As I lie there, my mind is crystal clear as I listen to multiple people in the room expressing themselves. What I am seeing and hearing is like a madhouse for the uneducated or newly indoctrinated like me. As I listen and watch for a while, I keep telling myself not to focus on what is going on around me, but to focus on myself. For some around me, their actions seem like a demonic purging. I keep telling myself, *"Not your journey, not your journey!"*

After waiting another 30 minutes, I realize that three cups won't affect me, so I go up to the front and ask for a fourth cup. The shaman once again asks me if I have laughed, cried, yawned, or purged out of either end. Again, I let her know that I feel completely sober and no purging has taken place.

She asks me, "How do you feel . . . IN your body?"

I check in with myself and notice a slight buzzing or vibration throughout my body. She tells me that this is a good sign and hands me my fourth cup.

After I state my intention again and take my fourth cup, I walk back to my mattress and lie down.

After a minute or two, I hear a voice in my head say, "Take a fifth cup."

I reply to this voice in my head, *"I just took a fourth cup, so let's wait to see what happens."*

As I lay on my mattress, this voice becomes more present and more insistent: "Take a fifth cup!"

After several minutes of back-and-forth with this voice inside my head, I get up and talk to the shaman, as I am becoming irritated by hearing the multitude of others purging and arguing with this voice. I tell the shaman that I have a voice in my head that keeps telling me to take a fifth cup of medicine.

I am certain she will think I am acting crazy. But this information doesn't faze her at all. It is almost like she is expecting it. This time, the shaman asks me to stand on one foot to ensure I was still stable and not feeling 'drunk.' I easily perform this task. Afterward, the shaman asks me again what I am feeling in my body. I let her know that the buzzing feeling I felt before is getting stronger, and I am starting to see tiny points of light emanating from everything around me.

The shaman tells me, "Very good! Bueno!"

She turns around and opens her medicine bag. In the bag is a vial with an eye dropper for a lid. She opens the bottle and adds a few drops of something to my cup in addition to the ayahuasca. She sets my cup of ayahuasca on the altar that is behind her. She proceeds to chant to the cup for a considerable period, easily a minute or two.

She picks up the cup, turns around, and hands me the cup. As she hands me the large shot glass filled to the brim with ayahuasca, she tells me, "I have a message to give you after you drink the cup."

I take the cup from her, and I say my intention out loud once more: "Show me who I have become!"

After I say my intention, she puts her hand on my left shoulder, leans into me, and tells me, "You will probably feel the effects of all of the cups at once. Enjoy the ride!"

As she tells me this, I find relief from my irritation, but it is replaced by a little anxiety about the unknown ahead of me. I walk back to my mattress, lie down, and put on my eye mask.

She was absolutely right! A few minutes later, I quickly went under the medicine and began my first ayahuasca journey.

As I begin my journey, cartoon-like images appear before me, even though my eye mask completely blocks out any light. I begin to see amazing, beautiful scenes and colorful shapes appear in the blackness before me. The images or scenes I am shown appear before me as though I am watching an animated movie.

At first, I see a beautiful meadow with colorful flowers and the leaves on the trees dancing in the wind. The setting sun casts a warm, yellow glow over the scene. This scene brings me warmth and peace. Next, I am shown a carnival-like atmosphere where joyful people laugh and express love for one another. These cartoonish people are blissful and present with each other, which creates an inward sense of connectedness to those around me and to the universe.

These scenes, all filled with love and exuberance, keep shifting from one beautiful, joyous event to another every 30 seconds or so. With each passing scene, all the participants and characters are in a state of pure joy, happiness, or bliss, which puts me in that state of mind as well. I do not recognize anything in the scenes as relevant to my own life.

I remember thinking, *"This is going to be amazing!"* as I began to fully relax and enjoy the show.

With each scene change, the time between scene changes starts to compress. Twenty-nine seconds, then twenty-eight, twenty-seven, twenty-six . . . and so on until there were about fifteen seconds between changes of scenes.

Next, I start to feel a blissful body sensation which feels like something moving around inside of me. Some refer to ayahuasca, or Mother Aya, as the vine of the soul. For many people, myself included, she manifests as a snake, either visually or physically in your body. She manifests as a small snake in my body that slithers around inside of me. They taught us in class that Mother Aya needs to get to know you before she can work on you. Since your trauma is stored in your tissues, she must crawl around your body as she does this.

In this moment, my body feels like a pond, and Mother Aya is a small snake swimming around inside of me. I think how weird it feels to sense the energetic flow moving through my body with such accuracy that I can pinpoint where she is and where she just left. As Mother Aya moves through me, my body feels energetic ripples flowing off her like a wake.

As she swims around inside me, the scenes shift from nature and people to mandalas. I see beautiful colors and geometric shapes meld and shift as though I were traversing an amazing kaleidoscope. After a few minutes, the feeling of her moving around inside of me begins to feel really good . . . I mean, really good! In fact, as she swims around inside of me, she begins to touch parts of me in a way that, to be perfectly honest, turns me on sensually. Her touch is very loving, like what tantric foreplay with a loving, tender partner feels like. As she moves around inside my body, she is tickling and caressing my most intimate parts in a very gentle and loving way. At this point, I think that she is probably slithering around among all the other fifty people in the room at the same time as me.

I giggle to myself as I have this thought and say to myself, *"I don't care if she is. In fact, I want everyone to have the same amount of bliss I am experiencing. Wow, Mother Aya is my new kink!"*

Shortly after I completely surrender to the visual and physical bliss she is putting me into, the time between visuals shrinks to a second or two between scene changeover. At this point, my mind and body are in such a complete state of bliss that words cannot fully or adequately describe it other than: This is the best I have mentally and physically felt in my entire life. Mother Aya is such a loving mother.

This is when she turns on a dime. Instead of showing me beautiful, peaceful images, she shows me my past!

She shows me scene after scene of my childhood, of my actions in the military, and of the hurt, pain, and death I have seen or been a part of. The only way I can describe this moment is that it feels like a 'life review' that Near-Death Experiencers (NDEs) describe. Only this was a life review of all the injustices I had seen or been part of.

When the first traumatic image is shown to me, I am completely taken off guard. I am like, Wait . . . what? I recognize this from when I was a young child, and it happened in my parents' bedroom. I am in such a state of bliss that as these one-to-two-second short clips appear to me, I am not able to fully grasp the memory but only feel the associated emotions before the next scene pops up to replace the last and grabs my attention. Just as I begin to remember what the memory was, where it happened, or how old I was, Mother Aya completely changes the scene and shows me another memory in a completely different setting, from a different time in my life. This rapid-fire video-clip montage of traumatic memories accelerates to the point I can't keep up as I become emotionally overwhelmed. My extremely blissful mind and bodily euphoria shift—and shift dramatically!

I rapidly begin to feel nauseated . . . and dark . . . and heavy!

My body wells up with nausea and intense pain. I go from complete mental and physical bliss to extreme discomfort in less than a minute. A pain in the pit of my stomach rapidly boils to the point I can no longer take it. I take off my eye mask and gasp for air. I get up from lying down because the pain in the pit of my stomach feels like a giant knot that is being pulled on from both ends: like a game of tug-of-war with no winning side. I crawl to the foot of my bed, where my white bucket is located.

As I arrive at the foot of my bed, on all fours, and look over my bucket, the knot in my stomach has formed so tightly that it is excruciating and not letting up! The last time I remember having a knot in my stomach that was even close to what I am feeling currently was the time I had to land my helicopter during the storm at night, and I thought I might die. I can tell that my body wants to expel this pain, but my mind or ego is refusing to cooperate.

My ego is telling my body, "We've got this! We can get through this without purging," and "We can overcome this! We can make it go away without letting it go."

For the next few minutes, my mind and body are in a brutal tug-of-war. As this internal battle rages inside of me, I hang my head over my bucket. My ego is trying to remain calm and soothe this pain, but the cauldron of boiling anger, resentment, hurt, fear, and sadness in the pit of my stomach isn't going to take "no" for an answer.

As I am down on all fours, staring into the bucket and waging this powerful, painful internal battle, a lightworker monitoring the ceremony begins waving a fan to cool me down. By this time, I realize I must purge for my own good.

I tell myself, *"Let it go! Let it go!"* But for some reason, I can't find the power or skill to untie the knotted pain because the weight of the dense energy that surrounds me was so heavy and constricting—it feels suffocating!

I take a moment to look around me. I notice several lightworkers around me purifying the air with smoke from the embers of Palo Santo. These coals are taken from the sacred fire that burns during every ceremony. I think I may even see the shaman around me. They are chanting as they wave fans to cool me while sprinkling me with their special waters. Their chant swells and strengthens!

At this point, I feel a powerful force and light energy surrounding me. It feels very cool and comforting. It seems to relieve me of some of the heaviness and darkness that surrounded me. As the energy around me lightens, I can feel the knot in my stomach loosening a bit. As the knot begins to slip, I do what they instructed us to do in class. I focus on breathing and surrendering. The positive energy from the shaman and indigenous lightworkers chanting around me, and the breathing techniques they taught me, allowed me to relax enough to surrender.

I purge, and I purge hard!

When people ask about my ayahuasca experience, they want to know about purging, as this is what many people fear the most. I can tell you from my own experience that letting loose and purging was one of the greatest reliefs I have ever felt in my entire life. To release whatever Mother Aya had rooted around for and found stored inside of me was extremely exhausting, but also completely freeing and enlightening.

I was so grateful to purge, and I am still extremely grateful to have purged.

Anytime I saw someone purge the following nights, I sent them my love, as I had so much respect for the inner work that they were going through.

I would think, "*You are doing great work, and congratulations for getting that out of you. Well done! Bravo!*"

A journey under ayahuasca is a rite of passage, and until you have been through a journey, you probably can't imagine how watching someone else violently puke can bring you joy for them, but there I was doing exactly that!

Additionally, I am also so, so very grateful to the shaman and the lightworkers who helped me release. They brought truly amazing energy to the process, which cannot be overstated. The shaman's wisdom and all the lightworkers' compassion as they facilitated our journeys are truly divine work. I am not sure I could have done it without their love and support, and for this *I will always be grateful*.

As the book *The Body Keeps the Score* describes, trauma can rewire the brain's basic wiring. Ayahuasca, as well as other psychedelic medicines, under the proper care, supervision, and integration, can facilitate a change to the score or rewire the brain and body to a better, more favorable outcome. For me, ayahuasca helped to release my pain and anger, and to reset my nervous system and default programming to a more relaxed stasis, and to open my most protected part of myself—my heart. Ayahuasca and the teachings of trauma-informed experts have shown me that it is better to release these negative thoughts, feelings, and emotions than to repress or hold onto them, as my mother had unwittingly taught me and as I watched my father do when we left my grandfather's house for the last time.

This is a pathway toward a happier, mentally healthier version of yourself.

While purging is preferred to not purging, I would offer that one should try not to verbally or physically purge their pain on another human being. Negative energy, when screamed at another, has a ripple effect and will amplify the negative, hurt, and pain. This is where that senior Marine officer failed that day. When he screamed at the doctor who saved an enemy combatant's life, he was letting go of some of his pain, but in the process, he put his pain onto another.

I hold no judgment toward this officer. In fact, I have complete empathy for what he was feeling and how he was feeling at the time. I know this officer is a good human who truly cares for those under his authority. In fact, he cared so much for his fallen Marines that a part of him died that day as well: It was obvious to see! The best thing for him to personally do this day was to scream it all out so he did not embody his pain, but unfortunately, he put his pain on another.

These stored-up, unprocessed emotions cause humanity to behave destructively. When our emotions explode onto others, it is because they become overwhelming for the individual and must be let go of. These repressed or stored-up feelings of inadequacy, shame, guilt, or whatever you are holding onto are what cause you to act in ways that are not true to your highest or most pure self.

We are hardwired to remember and store these negative events because, in the natural world, life is mostly peaceful. We, as a human race, need to do a better job at understanding our hardwiring and how modern life has created a bio-psycho-social environment that, for many, is toxic to our mental health. For too many of us, fear or a lack of safety is an all-too-common state in our daily lives.

By finding ways to release our stored negative feelings or trauma in a method that does not spread and spill over on others, we can begin to break the cycle of pain and anger that has plagued humanity for generations—and plagued me in my own life.

Psychedelic medicine can facilitate a new mindset or *perspective*. By releasing the grip that past traumatic experiences hold over a significant portion of humanity, we can reverse the hurtful cycle humanity has been in for many generations. These unresolved disturbances, traumas, and triggers are what cause unprovoked attacks on others. These mental health dysregulations are at the root of mass shootings in schools and public places. These people are holding onto their disturbances because they are alone and without the mental health tools to help them gain a new and better perspective.

We need to have compassion for these people, and we need to be kind and considerate to everyone we encounter to lower the social temperature instead of feeding the negative feedback loop so many of us are caught in . . . and our political leaders and media are so keen to use against us.

We need to ensure that people who undergo these powerful medicines are provided with an appropriate, safe environment and post-experience integrative support. This is a very important aspect for mitigating any dangers that these disturbing memories can pose. The retreat center I visited for ayahuasca offers a post-visit integration program for those who struggle after their visit. Additionally, the Wholeness retreat I attended over a year later had a team of professionals at our disposal should we have difficulties integrating our experiences. I was fortunate enough to be able to lean on trained mental health therapists in my area to help me process. Unfortunately, none of these professionals had any psychedelic training due to the current U.S. laws. So, in essence, I was guiding them as they were guiding me.

Ayahuasca and other psychedelic medicines can be very difficult journeys that can take weeks, months, or even years to fully understand and integrate their teachings. It has been over two years since I first journeyed under its effects, and I am still gaining new insight into my life from these powerful medicines. (More on this later.)

Dr. Gabor Mate's *The Myth of Normal* examines how modern life has dramatically shifted our normal from our ancestral past. For many of us, this 'toxic normal' has shifted us out of our parasympathetic side and into the sympathetic side of our autonomic nervous system, which reduces our natural ability to heal and learn, thus manifesting as mental and physical diseases. If we are to get healthier as a society and species, we must shift back to a more rested, relaxed mental state so our bodies' natural healing mechanisms can work optimally, which, in turn, will allow us to behave better.

We need to honor and legally allow for all tools to facilitate processing our emotions and traumas. By having a controlled set and setting with proper protocols, we can create a safe space to purge without spreading negativity to others and adding to humanity's pain. This is what psychedelic medicine did for me and why I advocate for the U.S. DEA to reschedule these powerful medicines down to Schedule III or IV to ensure that these medicines are legally allowed to be researched, administered, and treated with the reverence and respect they deserve. This includes reverence and respect to the indigenous people who have carried this wisdom for humanity for so long. They need to be included in the equation of prosperity that these medicines offer.

There are so many people in this world who have had significant traumatic events happen or have repressed or unresolved emotions that have built up to the point they are no longer able to be their best versions of themselves.

Hurting people hurt people. This does not make us bad people; our unresolved pain and suffering, not our souls, drive us to hurt others. Our soul, our most pure essence, our highest self, is love!

This I Know!

29

MY FIRST KETAMINE JOURNEY

Ketamine provides perspective by altering brain activity and enabling rapid neuroplasticity.

In June 2025, well over a year since my last psychedelic experience, I attended the Multidisciplinary Association of Psychedelic Studies (MAPS) Psychedelic Science 2025 international conference in Denver, Colorado. I attended the conference to compare my experiences with the latest research on the subject as I wanted to ensure I did not misinform, as I told my very personal story.

A regional wholeness center for mental health held a giveaway to one of their international retreats, which used psilocybin and Ketamine as their medicines. By the grace of God or spirit guides, I won the trip.

At this point in my healing journey, I was not interested in doing any more 'deep dives' with psychedelic medicine, as I felt I was still trying to process what had already been shown to me. Upon learning that it involved Ketamine, I was not all that interested because of my own misperception of the medicine. I can tell you I was wrong, and that it was a very soft, gentle, and lovely experience. This is what I experienced under Ketamine the first time.

Inside the ceremonial maloca, we were instructed to put the Ketamine Troches our mouths to dissolve but not swallow. As we sat with the medicine in our mouths, the therapists took turns reading to us beautiful passages while playing soothing music in the background. The curated flow of the experience was calming, while sparking curiosity, which set up for a very gentle and lovely experience. Once the allotted time of swishing the medicine in our mouths had past, they had us spit out the remaining medicine and lie down. Within a minute, I found myself quickly under the medicine,

As I drop into the experience, I found myself dropped and immersed in an energetic ocean; only I wasn't a human floating on top, but I was under water, and part of the sea. I found myself in the shallows but just below the surface, maybe 20-30 feet. I could see the surface above me and see the stirring of the waters around me and above me. I was not afraid or gasping for breath, because I was not human. Breath was not what I needed, because I was a part of all the waters and the waters were all part of me. Connected, supported . . . relaxed. As I observed the feeling of being moved by the current, I realized that what I was floating in was not ordinary water but water that contained all my feelings and emotions.

As I was floating in these waters, I would bump into various emotions, like sadness, loneliness, or gratitude. I would instantly recognize and deeply feel the emotion. If it was an emotion I did not like or did not feel comfortable with, I would try to repress it or move away from it, but I couldn't, as I had no means to move; after all, I was just a part of the sea and not separate from it. The more I tried to move away, the more it overtook me and carried me, like a surfboard catching a wave, only this wave took me to shallower and more turbulent waters. It would pick me up and carry me like a giant emotional wave until I was being tossed and turned. The waters were turbulent, throwing me around, leaving me feeling I had no control. The more I tried to resist, the faster it carried me, and the more disorienting or tumultuous it became. The waters around me became so rough that I had to let go. Once I did, I returned to deeper and calmer waters. I would ride my emotions like waves crashing onto the shore.

The emotions I felt comfort in, like gratitude or love, would pass through me only for a moment, and I somehow could not ride those emotions toward something greater as I had with the emotions I tried to repress or deny. As soon as I felt something wonderful, they flowed through me and were quickly replaced by another emotion, like unworthiness or guilt. Unworthy to feel something so wonderful because I did not deserve to have that feeling, because I was programmed at a young age to believe so. As soon as I felt unworthy, I found this feeling would pick me up and carry me back into the shallows and into disturbed waters, which would tumble me around until I had to let them go as a means of protection. I realized that the emotions I would try to repress or dissociate from stayed with me and became part of me, which only served to take me away from what I wanted or truly desired, and the emotions that gave me comfort and peace seemed to flow through me in an instant. When they were gone, and I did not know how to get back to them, as all the emotional waters looked the same.

I now understood why I could never seem to find or have long-term happiness or love. It was because I felt unworthy of those feelings, as the imprinting or programming of my youth taught me that I was not deserving. I learned early that I needed to be hypervigilant to the next destructive wave, and I prepared to be tumbled by the next storm surge. To relax and enjoy peace seemed dangerous to me. Instead of being in the calm, peaceful present and taking in the love, connectedness, or happiness around me, I let them wash over me and out of me before I could embody them.

I was born into stormy waters, which tossed me around, so this is where my mind or consciousness was focused on. These stormy waters made me focused and hypervigilant to the next storm surge, as a means of protection, as I had not yet learned to let them flow through me and out of me because my parents had not figured it out themselves.

I noticed that as I allowed the emotion to flow through me, I was able to move myself to calmer waters. The more I honored the emotion, the less it tossed me around. The more I held onto it, the bigger the wave became. Negative emotions are not dangerous if we learn to feel them, honor them, and express them in ways that do not harm others. It is when we hold onto them through rumination, repression, or denial that they carry us into dangerous waters, causing us to lose control. Bottom line: the more I try to repress or control my emotions, the more it affects my peace and calm.

It was a beautiful journey.

What we Resist, Persists.

This I Know!

30

INTEGRATION

Psychedelic integration is the process of reflecting upon and making sense of a psychedelic experience, and then integrating those insights, emotions, and experiences into one's daily life.

Integration is the hardest part of any psychedelic experience due to the requirement to let go of things which do not serve you. Patterned behavior and the default neural patterns that may have been engrained since childhood can be powerful forces which cause one to slide back. The neoplastic window that occurs after any psychedelic journey closes over a couple of weeks to about 1 month. Use This Time Wisely!!

I would love to tell you, the reader, that my life, is all rainbows, waterfalls and unicorns. Unfortunately, I cannot. All psychedelic journeys are unique and may require cognitive help to understand what was shown to you. If you take the time and devote the energy to yourself to find meaning then you will come out of the experience with new insights, not only in yourself but in those you have witnessed. What you choose to do with this knowledge is up to you.

Integration is a lifelong journey that requires routine, frequent check-ins with yourself to examine how you react or behave toward others. . . or toward yourself. I still battle with having and holding meaningful relationships and I recognize that I may struggle with this my entire life. In other words, I still have parts of me which are still tender. Now, I provide myself compassion and forgiveness, something I couldn't do previously. I realize that I am merely a preschooler when it comes to these things called emotions and feelings., You have to start sometime and you have to start somewhere. The only time you truly have is the present or the Now.

I still routinely tell myself to "be the best human I can to myself and others" as a reminder of how far I have come and how I want to show up every day. Integration is probably the hardest yet most rewarding part of the journey. Please visit www.aboynamedpooh.com/help for additional information on integration help.

Integration of inner cognitive trauma resolution may require radical treatment solutions, as the ones I have described, or may be accomplished through traditional mental health practices. At its very core, resolution will require the acceptance that some things that happened in the past were not okay and never will be, but that you are okay NOW!

Treat yourself to time devoted to understanding who you have become. Care enough for yourself to revisit old traumas and wounds so you can gain better insight and broaden your *perspective* on how they may be negatively affecting you. . . now. It is the knowledge and emotional control gained that make the past a place of reference, not a place of residence.

Subconsciously knowing that you and the world around you are okay, and having the mental resolve to respond in the present rather than react from the past, is an amazing gift you can give yourself.

This I Know!

SECTION III

'SHAKES' TAKE

This section is devoted to lessons learned, and tools and techniques that have been valuable in my transformation or healing process. As I state throughout the book: *This I know*! These are my personal truths, which may run counter to yours. "*What is mine is mine and what is yours is yours!!*" Please do not take offense at what I say. If the seeds of these ideas resonate with you, provide them with the fertile soil in which they can grow within you. By providing them with space to grow, you, too, can benefit from the blessings and lessons they have taught me. If they do not resonate with you, then let the seeds lie undisturbed and pay them no more attention, negative or otherwise. Know that what is contained in this section was written from a place of love and through love that these words are delivered.

Giant Hug!
Evan '*Shakes*' Holt

31

DRUG VS MEDICINE

A drug is a chemical substance that can alter a biological system, potentially having therapeutic or other effects. A medicine is a drug used to treat, prevent, or cure dis-eases. One provides short-term relief, the other long-term resolution.

Psilocybin, also known as 'magic' mushrooms, MDMA a.k.a. 'Molly' or 'Ecstasy,' or Ketamine a.k.a. 'Special K.' Are these illegal street drugs to avoid, to be afraid of . . . or are they medicines which can facilitate tremendous emotional healing of mental health conditions? The answer to both of those questions is a resounding YES. You may ask, how can two completely opposing questions both be true at the same time? The answer to which one is true depends on the 'Set & Setting,' 'Intension,' and 'Integration' in which the activity takes place.

'Set & Setting' are generally discussed together since they represent the immediate environment. Sometimes they are used interchangeably, but they are distinctly different. The 'Set' represents the 'mind-Set' or mental state of the individual when they consume or are under the effects of the drug or medicine. Whereas the 'Setting' is the external environment of the person while under the effects.

Let us first discuss 'Set.' The mindset matters when undergoing these powerful drugs or medicines. First and foremost, is your mindset to check 'out from' or to 'check into' your thoughts, feelings, or emotions? If you are using these medicines to check out, then, at best, these drugs will provide you with a stress relief valve, a fun time, and/or a weird perception of the world, which lifts your spirit in the very short term with some possible mid-term mental health effects. You will have a great little break from the 'real world' because the drug allows you to not think about your problems or the stresses of your current life, and allows you to let go of surface-level disruptions to your consciousness. At worst, these drugs can present very difficult challenges that, if appropriate safety measures are not installed, can cause significant harm to yourself or others.

The real 'magic' happens when the person uses these medicines to 'check into' their thoughts, emotions, feelings, or past difficult or traumatic experiences in an extremely safe environment. I recommend that you always 'check in' with yourself before consuming these powerful compounds. Are you anxious, nervous, or fearful? If so, try to soothe this aspect of your mental state regardless of your intent for consumption. The mindset is what establishes the starting point for the upcoming journey.

I have found that how I feel at the time of consumption is directly tied to the experience I have, especially when consuming psilocybin. If I am irritated, the irritation will become more pronounced. If I am feeling good about my day, the experience will be much more enjoyable. When I microdose psilocybin mushrooms, I can tell that it heightens what my body and mind are feeling *in the present*. This is exactly why I microdose psilocybin. As a person who can emotionally 'check out' or disassociate, repress, or ignore my feelings, I find that psilocybin connects me back to my feelings and back into my body, but only if my mindset is relaxed and I feel safe. In other words, they enhance my mind-body connection, and since the body keeps the score, this is a good thing if you want to process your trauma.

The next most important aspect of consuming psychedelics is 'Setting.' The setting is the external environment you are in when under their effects. It is extremely important that the setting be safe and positive. When the setting is safe and positive, this allows the hypothalamus in your brain to relax, shifting the autonomic nervous system rheostat toward a more balanced state or toward the parasympathetic side, where healing can take place.

Recent clinical studies have found that MDMA, for example, causes a greater release of serotonin and oxytocin, which are known to increase the human connection and stabilize a person's mood. *MDMA acutely increases parasympathetic activation while at th same time controls sympathetic activation.* This means the healing side is active, while the panic side is dampened. MDMA floods the person with feel-good hormones, putting the person's mind and body into a state of 'love' or safety, calming the person's regulatory and emotional network. For me, when visiting these difficult memories, I was able to see and to feel that a younger version of me was in a state of panic without being fully in the panic myself. This little bit of separation allows processing and, thus, release from its control.

This is why MDMA is very effective for the treatment of PTSD when used in conjunction with mental health therapy. One can revisit traumatic events without being strongly activated into 'fight-or-flight' or 'panic' mode, thanks to the sympathetic nervous system's control and the parasympathetic nervous system's activation. MDMA helps the person to maintain a balanced nervous system when revisiting difficult memories. By maintaining a balanced nervous system, a higher and broader level of brain activity and cognition can occur, allowing the person to view the event from a different perspective than when in an 'active panic' state, when parts of their brain get shut down.

When one does not feel comfortable in their setting due to a particular person, or action in their environment, this causes the person to be on alert or pushes the emotional autonomic nervous system into the sympathetic side. This turns down or turns off the ability to heal or cognitively process past events, depending on how far the emotional dial is turned into the sympathetic side. Safety is at the root of healing; thus, safety must be a key component to have any real, positive effect.

Should a real danger arise while under the effects of the medicine, your ability to assess and address it properly can be inhibited (medicine- and dosage-dependent). This is why the 'Set' (mindset) and 'Setting' (environment) are so very important to the person under the influence of these powerful compounds.

An unsafe set and setting can cause a bad trip, and these drugs can make an individual worse, not better. A bad trip can also happen while 'checking in' to your past because the nervous system can get overwhelmed while recalling a very traumatic event. This is much more common with psilocybin or LSD than with MDMA, as they lack some of the feel-good mood-stabilizing aspects that MDMA does. This is why I stress the importance of a very safe set and setting, combined with professional care. *If you have severe depression, anxiety, drug addiction, PTSD, or other mental health conditions, you should highly consider only undergoing these powerful compounds under professional care to ensure your safety.*

I only trusted myself with low-dose use of these powerful medicines and made sure I was in the safest set and setting I knew: my home!! Once I became aware of how powerful their healing benefit could be, I decided to do a deeper dive. I knew I needed professional help to ensure I had a successful journey. This is why I personally believe that these drugs/medicines should be regulated and their power treated with extreme reverence and with proper safety protocols. It is when they are sold through questionable or unregulated channels that variability in the compound's quality comes into play. When purchasing MDMA on the streets, one has to be concerned with other chemicals being added to the mix. Typically, speed, amphetamines, and methamphetamines are added to MDMA. This changes the experience the end user will have and greatly lessens its potential effectiveness as a mechanism to heal, since these chemicals lack the mood stabilization properties that MDMA possesses.

Regulation, in addition to protecting the quality of the compounds, also provides a legal means to procure the drug or medicine and to have more dosage options. Additionally, regulation establishes a vetting process that helps prevent those who would abuse their power while providing an easier pathway for those who would benefit. Lastly, regulation allows for additional research and education to be conducted openly to improve success rates by using the scientific method, which controls for various variables (dosage, in conjunction with therapy, as a mix of therapeutics, etc.).

For me to find success in the proper use of these powerful medicines, it took the documentary *How to Change Your Mind* to open my mind regarding the therapeutic aspects of using Schedule I drugs such as MDMA for the treatment of PTSD. Additionally, I was blessed to find a mentor who understood that one must take them intentionally to significantly increase their effectiveness. Both taught me to use these drugs as medicine and to 'check in' to my traumatic experiences, so I could honor and process the initial distress. I am forever grateful to have stumbled upon the proper use for maximum benefit.

I have known people who have gone to the jungle to do ayahuasca and have come back more confused, more dysregulated than when they left. I believe that the set and setting of being in a foreign country, in a strange location with unfamiliar people, can prevent the medicines from working because the participant is unable to feel safe enough to reach a physiological state of healing. Additionally, if the person does not have access to post-experience integration tools and support, the effectiveness of the healing medicine can be counterproductive, as it brings the distress to the surface but does not resolve it through proper integration.

Powerful psychedelics such as ayahuasca or Ibugaine, or the heroic journey of psilocybin, must absolutely be administered under the care or direction of qualified professionals, such as medical professionals, shamans, or accredited therapists trained in psychedelics. These people can ensure the 'safe container' is set through proper safety protocols, which ensure a safe and effective journey. Additionally, their skills as professionals in this space can help provide meaning or understanding.

My experiences have taught me that it can take multiple journeys and with different medicines in order to get down to and through our cognitive defenses. We are like onions with many layers of protection, so getting to the root of an emotional activation can be masked or blocked by other protective parts according to the Internal Family Systems theory. I know from my own personal experience and from observing others who were undergoing ayahuasca that a single or even a couple of experiences under ayahuasca can be very disorienting and can create significant emotional insecurities or discomfort, which requires talk therapy or integration sessions to make sense of what you experienced during your journey. Depending on how deeply repressed or forgotten some of your experiences are in your subconscious, it may require additional journeys under the medicine to fully realize or understand what is being shown to you. My three-year-old exiled part of me showed himself during a tarot reading after two light journeys under psilocybin and MDMA. Still, I did not understand what I had experienced or why until the next, deeper journey, almost five months later.

In the four ayahuasca journeys I took, each was completely different, shaped by the intention I set and by what had already been revealed to me. My first journey showed me how I had held onto, thus embodying a significant amount of trauma. My second journey created significant distress and discomfort, and if I had stopped after this journey, I would be worse off. This distress was resolved on the third night of medicine. If I had stopped at one journey under the medicine, I would have received a certain level of healing, which would have been beneficial. If I had stopped after two journeys, I would have been more disoriented and disturbed than before I began my ayahuasca journey. It took my third journey, when I set my intention to "Heal my heart," to solidify and integrate the love and compassion I was just beginning to show myself.

This I Know!

32

THE POWER OF PERSPECTIVE

Perspective is the way we see things. Depending on the angle or distance you view your past from, you will get a different perspective. Nothing is the truth nor a lie. Everything depends on the color or angle of the lens through which you view your experiences.

Internal Family Systems

Eight C's	Five P's
Compassion	Presence
Curiosity	Persistence
Courage	Patience
Clarity	Playfulness
Creativity	**Perspective**
Connected	
Confidence	
Calm	

Dr. Richard Schwartz's Internal Family Systems modality of psychotherapy uses the 8Cs and 5Ps to examine one's life. This chapter will focus on one of the Ps: Perception, and how perception interplays with the other Ps and Cs that form the foundation of Internal Family Systems terminology and methodology for understanding oneself. "We only know what we know when we know it" is a major theme throughout this book. For me, these words provided the compassion to forgive my father and to forgive myself, and are the words I use to explain how a lack of perspective can limit one's understanding of what is happening around them, to them, or by them.

There are always multiple perspectives that can be taken in any given situation or experience. You can take the perspective of a victim, hero, bystander, or observer, focusing on a single viewpoint, or you can holistically observe the entirety of the experience. What was I feeling and experiencing when I was being beaten? What was my father feeling when he was beating me? How did my siblings perceive what they saw or heard? Your perspective is shaped by what you have seen in the world and what conclusions you drew from the experience.

Dr. Gabor Mate states, "We may not be responsible for the way the world creates our mind, but we can learn to take responsibility for the mind with which we create our world." In other words, if we change our perspective on the world around us, we can gain control of the world we see and view it through a different lens than if we take everything at face value from a single perspective.

As babies and very small children, we absorb everything without much higher cognitive functioning, because we view the world at face value. This is the programming that we step into the world with. For any person with early childhood trauma, like myself, gaining perspective is a key ingredient toward healing. I have found that reexamining past events through different perspectives paved the way toward releasing the grip of my past painful memories and their emotional triggers.

For me, looking at my past with the idea of trying to understand my life through the lens of trauma created a different *perspective,* which opened my mind and allowed me to see my past differently. I invite you to take time to examine your perceptions of the world and how it has shaped your views. I challenge you to step outside your ego and view your life through a lens outside your own existence. Walk in the moccasins of another person and consider how their experiences may have shaped their ability to interact with you. Earlier in this memoir, I mentioned times when I was a teenager, sitting alone in my room. I discussed how I mentally struggled with questions about my father. I struggled with how my father was such an intelligent man but could behave in such a violent and destructive way . . . *and to his family, who he is supposed to love?*

When I ask this question again, as an adult and look through the lens of trauma, I can easily see what I couldn't understand so long ago. *It is the maturity of time and a deeper understanding of trauma that allowed me to perceive, thus understand, what I couldn't so very long ago.* If you're anything like me, your world will open up and your own life and actions will become much clearer.

In the words of Stephen R. Covey, "To change ourselves effectively, we first have to change our perceptions." One must first understand one's own paradigm, or mental map, and recognize that one's perspective is not reality, but a perception shaped by one's unique experiences and conditioning. What I have found with my limited use of psychedelic medicines is that they helped me to see beyond my ego and view my past with a different perspective, and therefore changed my understanding. With this newfound knowledge, I was able to come to acceptance and release the emotional pain I held onto.

As Dr. Bessel van der Kolk and Dr. Bruce Perry's work describes, "You must go back, and go in, in order to get through." I never fully realized how the multitude of traumatic events made me feel to begin with, since I learned to disassociate from my feelings at such a young age. This method only works well for small disruptions or ones that one can consciously remember.

By the grace of God or the guidance of my guardian angels, I was blessed to ask the right question, under the right medicine, which allowed me access to these dissociated memories. I was put in a safe container which provided me the ability to view my deeply troubled past without being triggered into significant panic, rage, shame, or disgust that would normally accompany these memories. In other words, I could feel the panic, but I was not 'in' the panic!! These medicines put my mind and body in a loving place, which allowed me to view these extremely difficult experiences with a new perspective. By separating the overwhelming emotions from the memory, I lessened the grip my emotions had on it.

Clinical studies have shown that MDMA keeps the higher cognitive parts of the brain active, so one can view their negative past with a fully active brain, which allows for better processing. When I viewed my past traumatic events with a fully active brain and a dampened emotional response, I was better able to process the traumatic events, thus releasing the emotional grip they held on me. In other words, I was able to lessen the emotional dis-ease as a result.

I am going to use a dream I had as an example of how one can view traumatic events with a different *Perspective.*

In early May 2025, I came down with the achy flu and a fever, and I stayed in bed for over twenty-four hours. At the end of this period, I had only what I can describe as a fever dream. During this dream, my fever broke, and I awoke drenched in sweat. I had a dream that walked me through my traumatic past as a young child.

In this dream, I was shown the multitude of times I was beaten as a small child with RAGE by my father. The way the dream presented itself was one of *curiosity.* In my dream, I was shown close to fifty times being struck across the face with a belt or similar rageful act. As I was being shown these memories, I was not emotionally attached to myself. In fact, as I was being shown these memories, I was not at all concerned with myself or how I felt. Instead, my dream focused on my father and what he was going through.

As my dream moved me from memory to memory, whenever I saw my father's face, time seemed to slow down tremendously, and all I could see was his face. This allowed me to focus on his eyes and facial expressions. What I saw in him every time he beat me was pain. DEEP PAIN in his eyes and face each and every time. I could see that the pain that made him so RAGEFUL was not what I had done, but what had been done to him so very long ago, and he hadn't resolved within himself. I could see that his rage stemmed from an unresolved past.

I awoke from my dream with tears streaming down my face. My tears were for my father because I had just witnessed his pain. Seeing our shared past through his eyes, I felt tremendous *compassion* for him. I wondered what could have happened to him to have so much unresolved pain that he could do this to his child. I will never know this answer, but I know his pain was deep and it was real!!

I felt so . . . soo sorry for him that he had to carry this burden for so long, and he was never able to resolve it in this lifetime. It was his unresolved pain that caused him to behave so badly and to abruptly end his own life. To be shown this so clearly in my dream gave me great comfort that my healing journey was on the right path. It was a beautiful dream!! Had psychedelic medicine been legally available and widely adopted, I believe my dad could have gained the perspective needed to resolve his pain and might still be alive today.

As a parting thought to perspective:

In the words of the song by Fia: The Art of Letting Go:

There are no mistakes,

I learn every day,

The universe is showing me the way.

We enter this world with a blank slate and learn as we go. Mistakes or imperfections are part of the human experience. *Be Kind to Yourself by letting go of mistakes. This has taken me way, way too long to understand its importance, but oh so liberating once I did!*

This I Know!

33

POWER OF POSITIVE AFFIRMATIONS

Repeating positive beliefs can reshape the mind toward a kinder, happier, calmer state, leading to increased motivation, reduced stress, and greater overall happiness.

Looking back, I realize that my morning affirmation of *"Best the best human I can to myself and others"* significantly helped me to transform out of my Wheel of Pain. I now realize that what you project into the world is reflected back at you. Affirmations do not change the world around you, but they change your *perception* of the world. Therefore, what you see reflecting back becomes different . . . better. If you can view the world more positively, then the world you see will reflect a more positive image to you.

Positive Affirmations, when done properly, are not about pretending things are perfect, but are words to remind you or inspire you to face and get through the challenges in your current life. Affirmations are a form of discipline that helps you be authentic and positive with yourself. They can help you to find and maintain focus, even when the world around you is bouncing you around in a storm. Affirmations help you reclaim who you are or who you want to be. Affirmations, when thoughtfully implemented, can give you the cognitive tools you need to better address the stresses in your life. By having the appropriate cognitive tools at the time, one can move through them, thus past them.

Affirmations work like water shaping stone; they work slowly and deliberately over time, cutting through the mental hardness that life imprints on all of us. When used consistently and for long enough, affirmations create new pathways of thinking and of perceiving the world. They begin by laying the neural pathways in our minds so we can become who we want to be . . . thus take control of our lives. I invite you to treat each affirmation like a seed you want to plant into your subconscious that will help you to treat yourself better or better respond to . . . (name your struggle).

By starting your day with a positive affirmation, as I do, you give yourself the best chance to have the day you want, rather than the day you dread. I have found that a morning affirmation lays the foundation for my day and better enables me to withstand whatever life throws at me. Over time, I am no longer just enduring life, but flowing through it with greater ease . . . and greater pleasure. This may require weeks, if not months, of repeating the same positive words to yourself.

Before I begin any challenging task or chore, I will stop and take a moment to ask myself, "How do I want to approach the difficult task? What do I need to make sure I am in the right frame of mind to handle said task? Is it *calmness, clarity, compassion, curiosity, creativity, confidence, or courage*?"

I sometimes tell myself I need to "address this situation with peace and calmness in my heart." I have found this quick reset of the mind sets me up for a more productive, less stressful, actual event. By doing this, I have become more productive and successful.

I sometimes tell myself multiple affirmations in a single day. Affirmations are not limited to one a day! This may seem like an overly simplistic exercise, but I have found that these daily patterns of reprogramming my thoughts were instrumental to my initial success and are an important factor to my continued success.

Affirmations can change not only your day but your direction in life. Dr. Joe Dispenza and his book *Breaking the Habit of Being Yourself* discuss in detail how one can retrain one's brain. Daily meditation, including affirmations, is a key aspect of his program to rewire your brain for a happier, healthier outcome.

Additionally, psychedelic medicine, due to the neuroplastic effects they have on the brain, can soften the mental hardness we develop over time. These medicines prep the mental soil, creating fertile ground for these positive seeds to grow. Like all seeds, affirmations need constant watering at the start to grow and take root in order for you to see results. If they are not repeated often enough, they will die or disappear, never to sprout into the positive life change you intended when you created them.

Should you engage in psychedelics to look inward, I challenge you to examine your life and find three to five affirmations you want to tell yourself. Make sure they are positive and would be what you would tell a close friend or family member who was experiencing the same difficulties you are facing. Write down or post these affirmations in a prominent location in your environment and make sure you repeat them at least once a day for the next two weeks to one month after each journey. I ask you to do this because the neuroplastic window that psychedelic medicines provide can close after a few weeks, depending on the medicine and dosage.

Before I microdose psilocybin, I always stop and think of something positive to tell myself before I ingest. I either say an affirmation I have memorized, or I think about something I want to bring into my life (peace, courage, patience, joy, calm), or something I need to let go of (procrastination, anger, anxiety) to address today.

Another form of affirmation comes through the music you listen to. Some of the best musicians have lyrics that cut through the noise and channel very deep emotions. Musicians like Bob Dylan, Adele, Toni Jones, Johny Cash, Eminem, and many others all have very powerful lyrics. Pay close attention to the lyrics of the music you listen to. Do they empower and uplift, or do they reinforce your anxiety, anger, or other negative thoughts or beliefs about yourself or others? I intentionally used lyrics from songs throughout this memoir so you could get a sense of the power of music and its lyrics. Additionally, I have curated a collection of songs and playlists on my website www.aboynamedpooh.com/music, featuring positive lyrics that I use to help me reprogram myself and maintain a happier, mentally healthier mindSET.

Sample Affirmations:

I will treat myself with kindness and love today.

I chose peace over . . . stress, drama, or . . . (fill in the blank)

I am in control of my actions and habits; therefore, I am in control of my life

I am going to treat today as an opportunity to serve and be authentic.

My thoughts shape my reality and, therefore, my path in life; pay attention!

What you resist, persists: What am I resisting?

Energy is reciprocal: Be Positive

Today I am going to focus on the Solution and not the Problem

I am resilient and open to abundance

My breath controls my emotions and health, breathe with intention.

I am going to live from a place that is authentic to myself

I am . . . (worthy, focused, powerful, disciplined, love)

I am so grateful to be alive, awake, and aware

I challenge you to create your own list and to make a commitment to say at least one per day for the next month. You will thank me if you do! A daily affirmation may seem like a very minor or inconsequential act.

Still, over time, my positive affirmations were able to cut through the negative self-talk that I found myself in. Therefore, I was able to create new neurological thought patterns, which made me a happier, more mentally healthier individual.

This I Know!

34

THE 'INNER' VOICE

"The Voice"

There is a voice inside of you
That whispers all day long,
"I feel this is right for me,
I know that this is wrong."
No teacher, preacher, parent, friend
Or wise man can decide
What's right for you--just listen to
The voice that speaks inside."
——Shel Silverstein

Listen to this voice. It is affecting your life in ways you may not realize. My voice has told me many things. It has helped me make the right decision when the right decision was not the easy decision. It also berated me for any mistakes I made. See, I had two voices stuck in my head. I had a voice that was guided by my heart. It was the voice that provided me with love and compassion. It protects and guides without judgment, shame, or guilt because this voice wants what is best for you. I call this voice 'The Divinity Within.' I also had my father's voice stuck in my head. This voice was much less kind or considerate. It lacked love and compassion because it was a *wounded part of me*. In other words, this voice caused me to overreact or behave in a way that did not channel the divinity within me. It wasn't until I met my 3-year-old version of me, who was trapped in time, and I showed him compassion, that this voice quieted, and I was able to see how much control it had over my life daily.

In fact, I did not even know it was part of me because it was so prevalent and pervasive, a constant chatter. Similar to living along a busy street or near a train line. I heard it so often that I didn't even recognize its presence in my life. This voice was where my self-limiting beliefs, negative thoughts, and emotions manifested from. This is why meditation can be so powerful. Meditation brings this part of you to the forefront, letting you hear yourself and the thoughts directing your attention.

At the ayahuasca retreat I visited, they call this 'the Split.' It is when one separates from their truest and highest self in order to survive or feel safe. It almost always manifests from a place of fear and typically fairly early in your childhood. Dr. Gabor Mate discusses how this split happens when you internalize a traumatic event or even a non-traumatic event, which your ego has difficulty resolving (distress without resolve or existential crisis). When you do this, you begin to separate your mind and your heart, or you start to lose your gut feeling. In extreme cases, it causes disassociation from your body completely (Rape or severe physical abuse, as was the case for me). You begin to disassociate or split from yourself. This is when many of us begin to engage in self-defeating behaviors as a mechanism for survival, for being liked or loved, or for placating the people or the chaotic world around us.

As you go about your day, I challenge you to be mindful of your inner dialogue. Listen to this voice to clarify your thoughts. This awareness can be extremely eye-opening and powerful to understand yourself, as it was for me. What are your internal conversations with yourself, telling you about yourself, the people you love, the people you work with, or are around daily?

Is the driver who just cut you off really an F'ing idiot, or are they simply distracted by spilling their coffee, or trapped in a disturbance inside their own head which made them less aware of the world around them for a short period of time? Also, see how long it takes you to get back to the mental state you were in just before being cut off or whatever emotionally triggered you. The longer it takes to get back to going about your day in a happy and healthy way, the more negative energy or emotions you are carrying, which can be likened to an emotional battery.

Ask yourself how you feel 'in' your body. Do you feel emotionally tired . . . or are you emotionally content? Are your thoughts or the people around you draining your energy, or providing it?

Understanding where the emotional leaks are manifesting from in your daily life is extremely important to being your best version of yourself. Are you beating yourself up through your internal dialogue, as I did, or are you absorbing the stresses of life and the negative energy around you? Either way, if you are feeling emotionally tired, this is where you need to focus.

Your emotional battery level provides you with the energy to engage with the world. When your emotional battery is mostly full, you have excess energy to give to others and take on the challenges of the day with vim and vigor. Vim and vigor are the energy and enthusiasm that provide you with the grit and determination to handle even the most difficult challenges. When your emotional battery is low, and you have the feeling that you are in a funk, or when it gets low enough or lasts long enough for depression to set in. Understanding where your emotional battery level is and what feeds it or drains it is very important for getting out of a funk or depression or for raising your vibrational energy level.

There is emerging scientific evidence that psilocybin increases mitochondrial function in your cells. Mitochondria are the power centers in your cells. Emerging evidence indicates enhanced energy production, reduced cellular aging, and mitochondrial biogenesis is a byproduct of psilocybin. My energy level shot up after three back-to-back light journeys at the festival. The emerging science seems to match my own experiences, which is another reason I still dabble in microdosing.

I challenge you to check in with yourself regularly to see how you're feeling or how your battery is. Being aware of how full or empty your emotional battery is gives you insight into yourself. It is this awareness or insight that will drive your ability to be productive or helpful to others. For those who suffer from high anxiety or are in an anxious state, you are carrying excess energy that needs to be let go of. Exercise, walking, or screaming (Preferably at no one) is a great way to release this excess energy. If or when you cannot exercise, I find piano music very helpful in downregulating my emotional state (anxiety). I combine piano music with intentional breathwork and/or walking to create a helpful combination.

When my emotional battery is low, I listen to upbeat music to counter my mood. I have several playlists on my website that are meant to uplift or calm the autonomic nervous system. I recommend you visit https://www.aboynamedpooh.com/music for inspiration. I use music to either motivate me when I am dragging or to settle back down if I am too energized. This has had a profound impact on my daily productivity. Modern life is filled with people and events that tend to drain your emotional battery . . . if we allow them to. Our political leaders and news media outlets use our emotions to our detriment . . . if we allow. They do this to take your energy or power away from you and fill their own with it. Your energy, like your money is a valuable currency, you should treat it as such.

If we do not take the time to routinely self-assess and care for our emotional capacity, our emotional energy slowly diminishes to the point where we start our day with less than a full charge. Similar to an old phone that now has only 90% of its available charging capacity due to its health having deteriorated. If you find yourself not wanting to get up in the morning, it may be because your emotional battery is not fully charged through proper rest, or because you spend too much time in a sympathetic-activated emotional state. If this condition persists, it leads to anger, depression, or other less-than-ideal behaviors. By routinely checking in and taking steps to address your battery level, you become aware of yourself (mind and body). This awareness brings attention, and if you honor what your emotional battery is telling you, you can set aside time and activities that charge it appropriately, or let go of people, activities, or news that drain your emotional energy.

For me, psychedelic medicine, specifically microdosing psilocybin, was a very important first step to rebuilding or recharging my emotional battery and removing the disturbances that prevented its charging. As I mentioned, I spent so much time on my sympathetic side, and I would check out from myself to the point my emotional battery was drained, which in turn was causing me mental and physical health problems. Very low doses of psilocybin allow me to check in with myself. Honoring my emotional state and nourishing the thoughts and feelings that arise allows me to resolve and let them go. Since unprocessed emotions do not weigh me down, I now have more emotional energy to deal with the present. Therefore, at the end of the day, I am left with more battery, and life does not seem to be as exhausting. Using psychedelics in conjunction with mental health therapy and self-reflection has been like replacing my computer processor with a much more efficient version, which takes much less energy to run and I can get through difficult processing quicker. In other words, I now have much more energy to deal with life.

You owe it to yourself to check in with your inner thoughts and feelings to see how the last day or week has made you feel, and how they caused you to act or react in any given situation. By doing this, you might find yourself better able to control your emotional energy as I have. You are worth investing this little bit of time in yourself, and if you're anything like me, you will find your world opening up to better and greater things.

This I Know!

35

THE DIVINITY WITHIN AND A HIGHER POWER?

If God created us in their own image, then do we not have God within us? Why not channel this positive energy within?

The problem I have with many organized religions is that they ask you to commit to and surrender to a higher power without an equal commitment to yourself. Some organized religions use this power imbalance to control their followers. They use it to maintain control, power, or a superior position relative to their followers. They make you believe you need them to become whole or good.

If you believe in a higher power, and I think we all should, I challenge you to believe in yourself equally. Believe you are good, believe you are worthy of love, companionship, and the community of others. Believe you have the strength to do your best every day. My mantra of "Be the best human I can to myself and others" manifested from a place when I felt the world was against me (happening "to me"). Instead of surrendering to a higher power and putting everything in its control, I chose to believe in myself (manifesting: "by me") and committed to being the best human I could be each day. It was my focus on and belief in myself that gave me the strength to do what I needed to act better, despite what my wounded ego was telling me or how the world seemed to be treating me. This, in turn, brought me closer to my higher power, since I was acting in better accordance with my higher power's divinity (divinity "through me"). In other words, one must act from the good that is within each and every one of us to ascend to the higher, happiest, healthiest version of ourselves ("as me").

I believe the higher power wants us all to believe in ourselves and to treat ourselves and others with kindness, compassion, and love, regardless of race, skin color, sexual orientation, or any other way we differentiate and judge others. The better we treat ourselves and others, the better we will lift each other up and overcome the hate, fear, and divisiveness that permeates our culture today.

For those who are struggling with how doing ayahuasca or psychedelic medicine fits in with their established religions or beliefs, I cannot answer this for you; every one of us has, or should have, a personal relationship with their higher power. What I can say with a high degree of assurance is that, whatever relationship you have with whatever higher power you believe in, if this relationship is healthy and nurturing, then your trust in its teachings will be solidified and emboldened by the ayahuasca or psychedelic experience. If your religion is failing you for whatever reason, then you will see these failings, and you will be emboldened to release yourself from the shackles your religion has placed on you.

If you fall into the latter category, do not despair, as your trust and belief in a higher power will be ever-present, and your connectedness to the divine source will be emboldened. For those who attended the ayahuasca retreat with me and did not believe in a higher power prior to their ayahuasca experience, they came out of the experience with an extremely strong conviction and belief in a higher power. To see them crack wide open was a blessing to witness. Ayahuasca, under the right set and setting, lifts the veil between your physical self and the energetic being (soul) you are. It connects and realigns the mind (ego) with our heart or soul. After all, it is a spiritual medicine. For many of us, we felt much closer to the divine. For me, it instilled a deep level of Santosha (contentment) that had escaped me most of my life.

The last tenant of the second limb of yoga is Isvara Pranidhana. Isvara, which translates as 'Supreme Being,' 'God,' 'Ultimate Reality,' or 'True Self,' and Pranidhana, which means 'fixing.' In most translations of this Niyama, we're advised to surrender to this Supreme Being or higher self, which, in essence, means cultivating a deep, trusting relationship with the universe and making each action an offering to something bigger than us.

My interpretation is that the higher power and True Self are one and the same, or at the very least, congruent, since ayahuasca showed me my divinity within. The highest Self one can achieve brings one as close as humanly possible to the perfection of God. This requires treating yourself and others with love, compassion, and kindness. This also requires that we strip away the pain, fear, abandonment, shame, guilt . . . that many of us have embodied and stored around our hearts as a means of protection. By releasing what no longer serves us, it opens up our hearts to a happier, healthier version of ourselves.

We must believe we are good . . . to do good. We must believe we are worthy if we are to accept good things into our lives. *Too many of us, myself included, have self-defeating behaviors and beliefs that limit ourselves. Limiting our love of ourselves limits our happiness and health. Once you let go of these behaviors and beliefs, your world will open up as mine has. We must all find a way to love ourselves, love others, and love our lives if we are to be a force for goodness and the light of God.*

This I Know!

36

REAL MEN DON'T CRY

Crying is a healthy way to process and release intense emotions, especially when feeling overwhelmed or stressed. It can help calm the nervous system, thus balancing it, which is responsible for relaxation and healing.

"Real Men don't cry" is probably the worst coping mechanism we men tell ourselves or employ. This mindset only reinforces the wounded masculine energy and behaviors. 'The Toxic Man' is behaving from a wounded side of the masculine energy. Are you acting aggressively? Are you insecure with how you feel? Do you blame others? Are you trying to control your partner's behaviors or actions? If so, you have some self-discovery to look into.

DIVINE	WOUNDED
Rational	Manipulative
Logical	Irresponsible
Grounded	Aggressive
Secure	Jealous
Courageous	Blames
Confident	Insecure

A great book that guides one on this journey is *The Inner Work* by Mat and Ash. This book does a great job of helping you to identify who you have become and what energy you are expressing. Are your behaviors magnetic or are they repulsive to those around you?

For me, crying was one of the first emotions I denied. Instead of crying and releasing the pain, I held onto the pain, which turned into anger. First, I became angry with myself. I was angry at myself for not seemingly being able to control my bedwetting. I was angry at myself for being a bad child who routinely disappointed my parents. By not crying and releasing, I channeled the emotion into anger toward myself.

Do you allow yourself to cry, or do you get angry when you are sad? Your answer provides you with a clue about your ability to handle, thus address and process, this feeling. If you don't allow yourself to cry or find your sadness turning into anger, you have some reflective inner work to do. Find out where this coping strategy initially manifested from and heal this part of you.

Crying can be and should be a very important tool in one's emotional toolkit for processing strongly felt emotions to sad or traumatic events. It should also be a viable release to strongly felt positive events, such as a beautiful wedding or an act of unconditional kindness. Crying is cathartic; it acts as a relief valve to release emotional pressure, lower stress hormones, and activate the parasympathetic nervous system: the side that heals!

Unfortunately, young boys are trained and taught not to express emotions. We are told that when we cry, we are being weak, or are acting like a girl, or are being a pussy. This only serves to begin the process of repression as a coping strategy; thus, we hold onto the pain of being vulnerable more than we would if we allowed young boys, adolescent teens, and men to feel comfortable enough to be able to cry. This culture of denying emotions is contributing to our male loneliness epidemic, as it prevents outreach or expression except through physical means.

As an American society that is mostly patriarchal, we allow girls to express their feelings to a much greater extent than we allow boys, or at least this has been my experience. Hence, one of the reasons women in the U.S. tend to be more emotionally regulated when it comes to crying. This being said, if you grew up in a family that was led by an emotionally wounded woman, your life experiences may have shown you differently. By shaming children for crying, we have been doing a disservice to our young men (and women), and therefore, they grow up to be wounded adults.

I cannot stress how important it is to understand and fully process our emotions, such as fear, pain, or hurt. By processing the emotion, we can attach meaning and thus resolve the wound. When we break a bone or receive a large cut, we immobilize and seal the area, and we give it time and the right environment to heal. Unfortunately, in the U.S., we do not honor mental trauma the way we do physical trauma; mental trauma remains with us much longer than it needs to. If one breaks a bone and it is not immobilized or properly reset, the person may lose mobility or function of that part. The same can be said of mental trauma. If we do not properly address the trauma, we lose our ability to cognitively address and respond appropriately to future similar events.

Unfortunately for veterans, first responders (Fire, Police, and Medical) and men in particular, we struggle to process our emotions associated with our sometimes-traumatic jobs. We are receiving small blows to our psyche on many days in a chronic way that go unnoticed because this is what the job requires, and our upbringing has trained us to look past or ignore.

For those of us who are in the business of traumatic events, we need to stop seeing the mental health effects of our jobs as a weakness; this mindset needs to stop. It is not a weakness; it is being human. It is OK for us to feel bad about the things we must do in order to preserve the whole. It's OK to be weirded out or a little queasy by some of the things we see or have done. For those of us who have partaken in the destruction that is a component of war, we must admit that it happened in the first place, we must accept our role, and we must learn to forgive ourselves and others to move past and heal the trauma that these destructive endeavors instill within us. The past needs to be a place of reference, not residence.

As a man who carried the wounds of my youth, I now see the challenges they created and the problems they caused. We only know what we know when we know it. Now that I see them for what they were, I can release them.

As I said, crying is not a weakness; It is being human. Crying is a mechanism our bodies use to release excess emotions. People cry at weddings because seeing such a wonderful display of love between two people can be overpoweringly beautiful. Crying is good, crying is healthy. Crying is a very important healing mechanism, and we need to allow ourselves the compassion to surrender to it willingly.

My unwillingness to cry was one of the major reasons my marriage almost failed. On Thanksgiving Day 2023, my estranged wife told me she had never seen me cry. She was right, I had only cried a couple of times in the 25 years we were together, and I would never allow myself to cry in the presence of others. She came to view me as a heartless human, and honestly, I can't blame her for thinking as such. Why wouldn't she think this? This is what I was outwardly projecting. My internal perceived strength was actually my weakness. The truth was, I was not heartless, but heartbroken and hurting, and had a scared little three-year-old exiled part of me locked up inside. It was the scared little boy inside me that told me it was too dangerous to have and honor this emotion because crying was not tolerated so many years ago. After all, as a child, the more I would cry, the worse the beatings became when my father was severely triggered when inflicting them. He probably received the same from his father, and he never resolved it; therefore, this poor coping mechanism was passed on as a generational trait. Locking up my ability to cry is what kept me from being a good human, first to myself and then to others.

My unwillingness to cry was what kept my anger, fear, and anxiety locked in me. It prevented me from expressing my love to myself and others. I never saw my father cry until after my mom had died. When he did, he bawled like a baby!!!! When I witnessed this, I did not see him as weak; I did not see him in a negative light. It actually made me see him as human, and it opened my heart enough to show him some compassion. Less than a year later, he unfortunately took his own life. I know he killed himself because he had bottled up too much trauma, too many feelings that, when they all came spilling out, they became overwhelming for him. He mentally could not handle and process 60 + years of stuffed pain, hurt, guilt. He could not provide himself with compassion and forgive himself for all the trauma he had caused to his family, so on August 19th, 2002, he used his Second Amendment right to end his own life.

Hurting people hurt people. My dad's inability to process and resolve his trauma is what made him who he was. He had complex PTSD, which came at a very young age and manifested as being a very emotionally dysregulated and angry human being. He saw his alcoholic parents fight over money, so he thought that if he could become successful, he could solve all the problems my parents fought over. He became a successful business person who provided for his family very well (economically). I never missed a meal; I always had nice clothes; and I was able to do any productive activity I wanted to engage in, for the most part. He was amazingly successful in this regard, but it was his emotional dysregulation that caused his life and those around him so much pain. It is also what caused him to end his own life way too early.

It was through his emotional outrages, stemming from an inability to cry and release, that he passed this repressed trauma on to his wife and kids as generational trauma. These repressed emotional traumas radiated out into the ones he loved, just like mine have done, and as all of us do! These unprocessed traumas rippled out and manifested as alcoholism in his wife as she tried to repress the pain she embodied for the pain that was inflicted upon us, as any good mother would do. Unfortunately, the emotional pain she carried became too much for her to bear and she ended her life as well. These unprocessed traumas of my father rippled out into his children. They manifested as alcohol and drug addictions in two out of three children, bipolar disorder, and other emotional dysregulations that are the 'normal' pathways for children of generational child abuse to take.

A critical component to healing from trauma is crying. I couldn't express tears in front of another until I had met the power of psychedelic medicine under therapeutic conditions. It took a couple of sessions of MDMA to allow me the softness for myself to reopen the channel to my heart and this pathway toward healing.

This I Know!

37

YOGA

The eight limbs of yoga are a comprehensive framework for ethical, physical, and spiritual practice: By uniting and integrating all eight limbs, one integrates fractured or exiled parts of oneself.

The body keeps the score. It keeps the score for physical trauma and mental trauma as well. Both make you more rigid and less flexible to absorb the challenges of life. Between the accumulated injuries from playing many sports as a youth, coupled with the physically demanding life as a Marine and stored trauma as a child, my body was hurting. I was in constant pain due to the chronic inflammation in my body. My sleep was suffering, I had gained weight, and felt 'over the hill.' After returning from the music festival, I decided to practice yoga regularly.

Yoga has been instrumental in uniting my fractured self: thus, my healing. I recommend practicing yoga if one wants to regain mental clarity, calm the mind, and strengthen the body. It also has the power to strengthen your connection to your SOUL: Source Of Unlimited Love, if all eight limbs are fully practiced. Yoga, by definition, means to connect or unite. It strives to create alignment and balance between Mind, Body, and Spirit (or Soul). Yoga, when done properly, empowers one to take personal responsibility and to steward oneself. For someone under significant stress, who has severe anxiety or exhibits signs of PTSD or Complex PTSD, yoga can be life-altering in a positive way.

There are eight limbs to yoga, with physical movement or poses as just one of them (3rd limb). In fact, the book *The Yoga Sutras of Patanjali* has 196 Sutras (Rules) . . . only three mention physical posture or poses. There is a lot more to yoga than vinyasas, downward dogs, or puppy poses. The poses are meant to incorporate or integrate the other limbs. This is why yoga is so popular in the healing community. Unfortunately, too many who practice yoga do not understand or practice the other seven limbs, which is why some have abused yoga in the healing community. I ask that, if you practice yoga, you open your practice to include all eight limbs. The true benefit of yoga comes from integrating and incorporating all the limbs.

Vinyasa yoga, also known as 'flow' yoga, is what I practice because it connects movement and discomfort with breath. In Vinyasa yoga, you sync your breath with movement. By syncing the breath with the movement, you are also syncing your mind and body, thereby regulating the autonomic nervous system. This syncing is very good for people who have trouble with dysregulation due to anxiety, PTSD, or another emotional dysregulation. *Breathing is your only direct tool to control your emotional state.* Breathing helps you manage the disturbances and distress caused by the difficult positions you put your body in. Once you do yoga enough to instinctively know when and how to breathe at each stage of a movement, you will find its rhythmic flow like dancing, and the breath cleansing to the mind and body. Where you once struggled with the movements you can lean into the disturbances and come to a place of calmness in both body and mind.

This ability to sync your mind and body through breath plays well in one's daily life as well. For those who have trouble regulating their emotions or find it difficult to push through or past emotional boundaries, yoga can be a tool to provide a pathway forward. I found myself able to recognize my emotional distress responses (triggers) sooner and with greater clarity. If I don't like where my emotions are taking me, I use breath to alter my mental state toward a more favorable outcome. The 'Ujjayi' breath, or ocean breath, is a slow and deep breath in and out through the nose. The sound the breath makes is like the waves on the ocean. It is a very soothing breath that helps when you feel yourself beginning to get triggered, or when anxiety or stress is starting to spike. Just like listening to the ocean waves, the ujjayi breath has a similar calming effect.

As you begin a yoga class, good instructors will have you clear your slate so you can meet yourself where you are in the moment and be fully present in the Now. For those who are constantly in fight-or-flight mode, being fully present can be a challenge in itself. The instructor will have you begin by standing, sitting, or lying still. They will instruct you to perform a particular breath, meant to center you in the present and prepare the body for the upcoming exercise. For extremely busy people, this helps bring your attention out of the past or future and connect your mind and body to the present moment. With the mind and body connected, one can truly be present with oneself.

Next, they will ask you to set an intention. Your intention can be to take something into your life (calmness, clarity, gratitude, connectedness) or, conversely, something that you want to release or let go of, which no longer serves you. (Anger, anxiety, annoyance . . .) If there is excess energy in the room due to people's busy work schedules, the instructor may ask the students to take a large breath in and out through the mouth (Ujjayi breath) to release this excess energy and center the students. This will be followed by some easy warm-up movements and stretching to prepare the body for the upcoming flow.

Once you are fully present and your body is warmed up, the main vinyasa sequences begin and are repeated equally on both sides to create balance. After you have gone through a difficult movement cycle and the body is starting to feel overwhelmed, they will encourage you to breathe in through the nose and rapidly out through the mouth to release excess energy and emotions. There are a few versions of this, but the most aggressive is the Lion's breath. This breath helps one to let go of the excess energy or disturbances that have built up in the body and mind. By letting go of this excess energy, you can return to a state of calm and control, thereby rebalancing your nervous system. In other words, it teaches you how to calm your nervous system when your body and mind are under stress/duress. This can be useful for those who suffer from panic attacks or find themselves in emotionally triggering events routinely.

Between sequences, you typically rest in either downward dog or child's pose. The importance of the child's pose or downward dog in the practice of yoga is to bring everything back together and return to calmness. Both positions are positions of rest and mindfulness. When in these positions, focus on the parts of the body and mind under duress, and direct your breath to that area to soothe the discomfort. In other words, re-regulate these parts of yourself.

At the end of the workout, they will have you lie in stillness so you can fully return to a state of calm. This is an extremely important aspect of the practice as it helps you to rest and digest (process and appreciate) the difficulties you just went through. The instructor will remind you to give yourself gratitude for the work you have done, honor yourself, and ask you to take this gratitude with you for the rest of your day.

This is exactly what many of us lack: gratitude for where we are today. Meet yourself where you are today, and each and every day, push forward to a better you. It is a very slow and deliberate journey. Still, if practiced routinely, it can have a profoundly positive effect on your daily stress levels and on your ability to regulate your emotional and nervous systems.

As you develop your yoga practice, you will find that through breath and exercise, you can take greater control of your emotions, mind, and body. I hope that you will find, as I have, that the stresses of life do not seem as troublesome. By controlling the breath, one can manage the mind and body's stress response in a calmer, more peaceful way. Yoga, when practiced properly, can improve your emotional intelligence when life seems to be blowing you around.

If you are anything like previous me, the mind can be very abusive when it has a disturbance in its consciousness. This manifests through beratement, anger, shame, judgment, anxiety, or similar negative emotions. It can also be very loving when in a state of calmness or gratitude. *Fun Fact: You cannot hold anger, resentment, or judgment . . .*

and hold gratitude at the same time. These emotions are not compatible. Life is so much better when one is grateful than when one is angry. Yoga helps me let go of the anger and other negative emotions that no longer serve me, and allows me to quickly return to a calmness that had previously eluded me, which leads me to find my gratitude.

As I mentioned, the poses are just one of the eight limbs. It is the physical practice intended to unite the other limbs. As I began educating myself about some of the other limbs, I realized I had subscribed to many of their teachings, even though I had never heard of them. The first limb, YAMA, refers to vows, disciplines, or practices primarily concerned with the world around us and our interactions with it. While the practice of yoga can increase physical strength and flexibility, what's the point if we are still rigid and stressed out in day-to-day life? I could go on and on about the various other limbs of yoga, but that is another book in itself.

Through practice and mindfulness, I have come to understand that our energy state is always changing and flowing from moment to moment. Having pent-up energy can be a really good thing when you are about to do some really hard exercise. But having pent-up energy when you are trying to go to sleep at the end of the day is not so good. Yoga helps one better align the mind, body, and spirit (soul) with what one's present environment requires. Yoga provides you with the tools to manage the ebb and flow of your energy state so that your energy state doesn't manage you. In the words of Dr. Gabor Mate, "We may not be responsible for the way the world creates our mind, but we can learn to take responsibility for the mind with which we create our world." Yoga has helped me to take responsibility for my mind and how I perceive and interact with the world.

This I Know!

38

TRAUMA AND GRIEF

Like physical trauma, mental trauma can be healed if you provide it the proper attention and care. Downplaying only serves to create scar tissue, thus limiting your recovery.

Traumatic events are what happen to you; trauma is what happens inside you. What I hope you take away from this memoir is that traumatic events (Big 'T' or little 't') happen to everyone . . . eventually. The effect of traumatic events on your current and future self depends on how deeply you process the emotional wounds that these overwhelming events present to you. Because these events are overwhelming, we store the emotions along with the memories, which can interfere with or dysregulate our future emotional responses. We embody these negative events and wrap our hearts with these memories as a means of protection. These negative life experiences can manifest into negative behaviors, which cause us to behave badly to ourselves (addictions, phobias, cutting) or others (verbal, psychological, or physical abuse). What separates one person from another is how well one has fully processed the traumatic events that one has faced earlier in their life. The better one has processed the traumatic events, the better one can let the past be a place of reference, not a place of residence. *The only way to remove the trigger, rush of adrenaline, panic, anger, sadness, etc., is to go 'into' and go 'through' in order to 'get out'.*

The children's book *We're Going on a Bear Hunt* is a great analogy for doing this kind of inner work.

In the book, each obstacle has an onomatopoeic description. Before each obstacle, the children chant the refrain:

> "We're going on a bear hunt.
>
> We're going to catch a big one.
>
> What a beautiful day!
>
> We're not scared."

Followed by (while crossing the obstacles):

> "We can't go over it.
>
> We can't go under it.
>
> Oh no!
>
> We've got to go through it!"

WE'VE GOT TO GO THROUGH IT is the only way one can resolve these triggers and wounded behaviors that reside in all of us. This is how we get back to the divinity within all of us. Some of these bears can seem insurmountable, while others can be extremely frightening to face, but don't be scared because once you get through, the bear is gone.

To be able to do this, you must provide yourself with a safe space, both physically and emotionally, in order to be able to let go of and resolve the emotions that accompany the events.

If revisiting the event causes you to become overwhelmed, then powerful medicines under therapeutic conditions may be required as they were for me.

If you take anything from this memoir, take the time to look inward and examine your upbringing and life experiences. Examine your most negative events through the lens of trauma, not only for yourself but for your parents, siblings, or other important people in your life. Armed with this knowledge, you can begin taking responsibility for how you see, therefore, create your world moving forward. If there are aspects of your behavior you do not like, this is normal and part of the human experience.

Do not suppress, shame, or hide this part of you. Instead, examine it with *curiosity* and *compassion*, as IFS therapy has taught me. Some of the parts of yourself may be very difficult to understand, accept, or even get down to the root of manifestation. Some of these parts may require outside help or professional care to guide you through experiences that have trapped a part of you in the past . . . as they did for me.

You are worth it, and I am rooting for you. In fact, I am giving you a giant hug and sending amazingly positive and loving energy your way so that you, too, can have the courage to go into your most painful memories, love, or radically accept your past so that those memories can reside where they belong -as a place of reference. By resolving your past, you will no longer activate these old wounds, allowing you to be a better version of yourself moving forward . . . as they have for me.

For those of us who either have Post Traumatic Stress Dysregulation (PTSD) or Complex PTS-Dysregulation, it may require a set and setting beyond what we generally can achieve by ourselves. This means professional help with powerful medicines may be required. Remember, it took extreme danger and emotional pain to cause the dysregulation to begin with. Therefore, it may require extreme tools that provide safety of the mind and body to release the stored trauma. Extreme safety of the mind and body is a necessary condition to remove the dysregulations that traumatic experiences can instill.

Should you decide to utilize psilocybin, MDMA, or other powerful hallucinogenic medicines on your own, I ask you to make sure you understand how important set, setting, intention, and integration are to the process. Make sure you do it in a highly safe environment, with proper safeguards and guidance. Make sure you take the time to integrate and provide yourself with love and compassion during this process. Many licensed mental health professionals can help you understand and piece together a psychedelic journey afterward, so help is available and becoming more prevalent.

As a very dear friend recently told me, "Trauma should not be downplayed," and he is absolutely right. It doesn't matter if you classify whatever is disturbing you as trauma or don't even use the word trauma. Just honor any unresolved emotional disturbance you hold onto and let them go. This is the only way I have found to move past their activations, which negatively affected my present.

We tend to downplay our own trauma. Because we downplay it, we often fail to fully recognize its impact or accept its effect on us. This coping mechanism causes us to hold onto the negative effects in our daily lives much longer than we should, because we want to show strength . . . when tenderness is what we need to offer ourselves.

By honoring the feelings associated with the negative event and treating these parts of us with tenderness or vulnerability, we can begin to fully release ourselves from our past. It is when we hold onto or repress our feelings that we embody negative feelings about ourselves or others, which builds a wall within and starts to separate us, first from others, then from ourselves. By unblocking the memories of the three-year-old version of myself, I removed the cornerstone of this wall and broke it down. This wall contained not only the bad, but unfortunately, it locked away the goodness within me that I was unable to share with those around me. It is an unfortunate side effect that cannot be escaped from, or at least I couldn't!

In the lyrics of the musician Trever Hall, "You can't rush the healing and darkness has its teachings." The Stoicism philosophy of Amor Fati shares this belief. Darkness does have its teaching, as I have recently found. If the darkness has fractured you, as it did me, you must be cognizant of this. Not as I did by telling a joke about how fucked up that one time was . . . but by actually looking at the event through different perspectives and sitting in the memories to see how you feel:

Mind-Body connection. If you start to get angry, shake, sweat, get chilled, or God forbid shed a tear . . . well, it means there is trauma left in your body and mind that you need to let go of: *Honor This!*

There are so many good tools, strategies, or modalities that can help you heal. Journaling to capture your raw emotions when they are the strongest or sharpest, music therapy, dancing, and humming to vibrate the Vegas nerve can help soothe a wounded part of you. Walking while talking with a friend or other form of EMDR therapy, which keeps you distracted enough to prevent the emotion from overtaking your ability to process. These are all great tools to help you in this regard. Finally, psychedelic medicine can be extremely helpful to resolve those parts of you that you have hidden even from yourself. Whether in low doses (microdosing) or at the other end, these medicines can be an important tool toward a happier, much healthier version of yourself, as they have for me. Psychedelic medicine, when used for therapeutic purposes under the right intentions, under the proper supervision and care, can do wonders for accelerating one's healing or transformation journey.

If you have made it this far, my only advice to you is to take from the book what resonates with you and plant the ideas as seeds in your psyche. Provide these seeds with the nourishment to grow. *The Power is, and always has been, within you.* Employ any of the tools that you feel may be useful for you to be your best version of your truly divine self. *We always find what we are looking for.*

This is why a drug addict can always find drugs; they are highly motivated to find them. I want you to find your happiest and most healed self so you can behave through the divinity within you.

What I want does not matter; it is *what You Want that Matters.* Love yourself enough to find out.

If you do not know where to begin this journey, I would suggest starting each day with a mantra or positive affirmation that empowers or inspires you to be your most authoritative and authentic self. This is how my journey began, setting me on a path toward forgiveness and *compassion.*

Next, ask yourself, "Is there anyone you cannot forgive, *yourself or someone else?"* If this question does not feel authentic, then look inside and ask yourself . . .??

Other modalities can serve as a companion to or an alternate starting point from who you are . . . today.

Remember, you are the one you are waiting for. *You and you alone* can fix yourself. *You, at your most authentic and purest self, are good.* Understand this and learn to forgive yourself and others. Purge your pain in private or only to those who are trained professionals or can hold this space for you, without taking on the pain as their own. You are enough, you are worthy of self-love and self-compassion. Remember that holding resentment or anger only hurts you; so stop hurting yourself!

Bottom line: if you fully process whatever negative life experience has presented you and you release the hurt pain, anger, or anxiety that you have stored inside you, then you will rise up into a happier, mentally healthier version of yourself, and . . . all that is left is love.

Hurting people Hurt People, but . . .

Healed People Heal others

Enlightened people illuminate others

And love always wins, so shine your light of love . . .

on all who may cross your path in life,

Because what you do matters

Spread only good seeds and love your fate.

With Love,

Pooh

PS: If you made it this far and found what I say useful, I humbly ask you to recommend this memoir to others or write a review. This book came about because I wanted to ensure that I did not let my blessing go to waste. It is through spreading the Seeds of Life that we all can do our part to help humanity heal.

With Gratitude,

Pooh

For additional information and tools, go to www.aboynamedpooh.com

ACCEPT YOUR FATE OR AMOR FATI

Love Your Fate or Amor Fati is a central idea in Stoic philosophy, emphasizing the acceptance and even embracing of everything that happens in life, including the good, the bad, and the indifferent. Rather than just enduring hardship or challenges, Stoicism encourages finding value and purpose in whatever happens, no matter how painful or unexpected. It was with this philosophy that I began my introspective look into who I had become:

Key Concepts:

Acceptance of Reality: Stoicism teaches that many things in life are beyond our control—death, the actions of others, or random events. What we can control is our attitude and response to these circumstances. Amor Fati encourages one not only to accept these uncontrollable events but also to deeply embrace them.

Fate as a Teacher: Instead of seeing life's challenges as merely negative, Stoics view them as opportunities for growth and wisdom. Adversity shapes character. In embracing fate, you also embrace the process of becoming wiser, more resilient, and more virtuous.

Freedom from Suffering: Resistance to what happens often leads to suffering. By loving fate, you align yourself with reality and free yourself from unnecessary emotional turmoil. You stop fighting against what is and start flowing with it.

Cosmic Perspective: Stoicism teaches that everything in the universe is interconnected, and each event has its place in the grand order of things. When you love your fate, you trust that whatever happens fits into this larger picture, even if you can't see how in the moment.

The Amor Fati mindset is both empowering and liberating. It removes the victim mentality and allows one to find meaning and strength, no matter what life throws at you. This book emerged from my embrace of the Stoic principle of Amor Fati and the sacred geometric pattern of the Seed of Life. So much so that I had them tattooed over my heart as I began my journey to 'Find Myself' beneath all of the pain and suffering I had been a victim of, witnessed, or caused. It is with these principles that I share my story

ACKNOWLEDGMENTS

To my loving wife and amazing two children, without you, I would be nothing. In fact, I might not have been alive to write this book without your love and support through the years. What I now know is that I was not any better than my own father in dealing with my early childhood trauma and pain. While I did not physically abuse any of you, I did put my emotional pain on you all. Additionally, I deprived all of you of my love and presence. Some of it was because I was routinely deployed around the globe and not physically there. Mostly, though, it was that I couldn't seem to break away from my past and be in the present with you all. It was my verbal anger and emotional neglect that left you all with emotional scars, and for this, I am very sorry! My mantra of "We only know what we know when we know it" seems shallow and does not adequately express my regret for the times I was angry, closed off, or dissociated to the point of not being present in your lives. I have always loved you all much more than I loved myself. This I KNOW!!!

I also feel so blessed to know what I KNOW NOW and still have you three by my side and still in my corner. We now have the opportunity to change the outcome of our family's future due to my newfound knowledge and understanding of my shortcomings. I can't wait for our next chapters as my heart is filled with love and joy, not only for you all but for myself as well. It is this love for myself that empowers me to show you the love and respect you have always deserved. It is my promise to you all that I cannot and will not go back to that angry, closed-off human being I once was.

To my mom and dad, I am sorry it took your deaths to make apparent how deep and painful your personal struggles were. Know that your fear and pain were not lost on me. It was woven into my heartstrings and helped make me who I have become. I am grateful to you both. My only regret is that we all couldn't have had the opportunity to do psychedelic plant medicine together, so that we all could live much happier and longer lives. I tell your stories so that others can learn from your experiences and avoid a needless, tragic end. I know your life stories would have ended differently if we could have broken the generational trauma that plagued our family while you were still alive. Rest in peace, knowing that some of the generational and traumatic ties that bound our family's ancestry have been released so that future generations can live freer and more fulfilled lives.

To my 3-year-old version of me: Meeting and seeing you, and all of your innocence, still blows my mind. Thank you for coming out of hiding and for sharing your experiences, thoughts, feelings, and emotions with me in such amazing detail. Seeing and feeling what you felt so very long ago truly opened my eyes to our past. You provided the foundation that allowed 'adult-me' to piece my life back together again. I will never forget the first hug and love I gave you after you gave me those memories back. To feel the understanding, the compassion, and the unconditional love that adult-me gave you poured back into the 'adult me' gave me everything I had been missing for 50 years. With this newfound love for self, I was able to look at other parts of me with love, compassion, and understanding that we had never been able to before. Thank you for trusting me with your most painful memories. Remember, It's Not your Fault!!

To my brother and sister: I now SEE YOU and better understand your challenges, how our chronically stressful home life affected you, and what drove you to make the decisions you did. I wish I could go back in time and be more supportive, but we only know what we know when we know it. Because our trauma is so intertwined, it has caused me to stay away, as it was too painful a reminder of what we went through and how it deeply affected us all. Know that I love you both with all my heart - Love Pooh

www.ingramcontent.com/pod-product-compliance
Lightning Source LLC
LaVergne TN
LVHW022159200926
848481LV00006B/1784

* 9 7 9 8 9 9 4 5 3 4 2 0 5 *